Dedicated to Jack Moore and all fly
fishermen who release wild trout

1992 printing

American Nymph

Fly Tying Manual

By Randall Kaufmann

Cover: Klamath River rainbow caught, photographed and released by Brian O'Keefe.

FRANK AMATO PUBLICATIONS
P.O. Box 02112, Portland, Oregon 97202

HOW TO BEST LAND AND RELEASE FISH

Do not release a tired fish until it has COMPLETELY recovered. Firmly hold a played out fish by the tail with one hand and GENTLY SUPPORT the fish from underneath just behind the head with your other hand. Face the fish upstream in an upright position in fairly calm water, but where there is enough oxygen to allow the fish to breathe easily. By moving the fish back and forth in this position the gills will begin pumping life giving oxygen into its system, while at the same time allowing the fish to rest and regain strength lost during the battle. Fish being revived in this manner will often attempt to escape BEFORE they are completely recovered. A good rule of thumb is not to let the fish swim away the first time it attempts to. When fish are released prematurely they will often swim out of sight, lose their equilibrium, turn onto their side and die. It doesn't hurt to revive fish a bit longer than you feel is necessary. This will insure a complete recovery without complications. This process usually takes a minute or two, but fish that are extremely tired can require several minutes. This is especially true preceding, during and after spawning periods. When you do release a fish, do so in calm water, allowing the fish to swim into the current at its leisure.

After releasing a fish, move slowly, for sudden movement may spook them prematurely. NEVER TOSS FISH back into the water. If you wish to take a photo, "set up" everything before you remove the fish from the water. Cradle the fish and lift it just a little above the water so if it should happen to fall, it will not crash onto the hard shoreline. Fish can also be laid on wet grass for a couple of seconds. Do not put undo strain on the fish by lifting it high or in an unnatural position. NEVER PUT YOUR FINGERS IN THEIR GILLS for this is like puncturing a lung. NEVER SQUEEZE fish as vital organs are easily damaged. Fish will seldom struggle when handled gently. A quick, harmless way to measure fish is to tape off measurements on your rod or buy a "fish tape" which adheres to your rod. Simply slide the rod alongside the fish in the water and you get an accurate measurement. Spring scales are deadly on fish and should only be used for hoisting

a net with the fish inside. It is easy to estimate the weight by the length and condition of the fish. The important consideration is to release fish quickly and unharmed. A fish which is bleeding slightly will probably survive just fine. Even a fish that is bleeding profusely can usually be revived if you are patient enough.

Try to land fish in a reasonable amount of time. The longer some fish are played the more lactic acid builds up in the bloodstream and the more difficult it becomes to revive such fish. Most fatal damage occurs to fish through improper handling, not during the actual hooking and playing of fish. It is best not to handle or remove fish from the water. When a fish is removed from the water it begins to suffocate immediately and the risk is great that it will flop about on the bank, slip from your grasp, or that you may unknowingly squeeze it to death. If you MUST handle fish, be certain your hands are wet, for wet hands will not destroy the protective mucous film on fish, especially trout.

To remove the hook, gently grip the fish by the tail or jaw with one hand, removing the hook with the other. If you are wading, both hands can be freed by slipping the rod into your waders. If a fish is hooked really deep the hook can often be removed with the aid of a long nose pliers or forceps. If not, it is best to cut the leader, leaving the fly in the fish. Nature supplies a built-in mechanism which will dissolve the hook in a matter of days. Oftentimes a friend can lend a hand in unhooking and reviving tired fish.

A barbless hook will help insure safe handling and facilitate a quick release. You seldom have to touch the fish as barbless hooks can usually be backed out very quickly using only one hand. Under specific conditions, a net, if used properly, can be a tremendous advantage, allowing you to quickly land and release fish. A net can alleviate fish flopping and thrashing over rocks in shallow water and can greatly aid you in landing a fish when you are waist deep in water. Be careful fish do not become entangled in the net.

About Barbless Hooks

This is the fifth season in which we are tying many of our nymph and dry fly patterns on barbless hooks. During this time many of you have written to us relating your own "amazing findings" that MORE FISH ARE LANDED WITH BARBLESS HOOKS than with barbs! Sometimes fish will escape but such instances have nothing to do with the absence of a barb.

There are only positive reasons for fishing a barbless hook. There are no disadvantages. More fish, especially big fish, are hooked on a barbless hook because they have a tough, bony mouth and hooks have difficulty "penetrating" or "sinking in" to the bend of the hook. A barb forms a wedge. Isn't it quicker and easier to drive a nail than a wedge? How many good fish have you "missed" on the strike, and how many of those would you have hooked if the hook point was sharp and the barb smashed flat? Remember the last time you had a good fish on and the line suddenly went slack? Chances are the hook never penetrated and just fell out of the fish's mouth. The fish was never hooked . . . you were!

We have tested barbless hooks on all varieties and sizes of freshwater gamefish and our findings show we hook twice the number of fish on barbless hooks. You don't think we fish barbless hooks because

we like to lose fish, do you? Pull a barbed and barbless hook into a piece of cardboard, you'll see and feel the difference. When a hook sinks to the bend of the hook, instead of only part way, you have the fish until you back out the hook exactly the way it went in, or until it breaks through the skin.

Remember the last time you hooked your clothing or skin? Avoid the pain and frustration, smash those barbs! The best way to debarb a hook is to smash it flat using a flat nose pliers. Be careful not to damage the hook point. Fish are most often fatally damaged during handling. A barbless hook allows you to release fish easily and with a minimum amount of handling. Usually you will not even have to touch the fish. In Alaska we tested the fishing speed of barbed versus barbless hooks. The angler fishing barbless hooks was able to release nearly twice as many fish as the angler fishing a barbed hook! The time consumed in handling fish, working out the hook with pliers or forceps and the time needed to properly revive fish handled in such a manner, drastically reduced actual fishing time . . . and the catch, not to mention the possibility of damage to the fish. We are confident you will find barbless hooks a pleasure to fish.

Contents

Randall Kaufmann

About the author:

Randall Kaufmann, and his brother, Lance, operate a full service fly shop in Tigard, Oregon. They also publish an illustrated catalog of fly tying and fishing equipment. Kaufmanns' Streamborn Flies, P.O. Box 23032, Portland, Oregon 97223, (503) 639-6400.

Acknowledgements

I WOULD like to thank all those who have shown an interest in this book since its inception – especially Frank Amato, my publisher. I am also grateful to my brother, Lance, for his fine ideas, invaluable help and encouragement. Special thanks go out to Dick Wiegand for his fine illustrations and to Bill Berg who lent his talent to get me started with the photographs.

Also, thanks to my wonderful parents, Jack and Oda Moore, for all their help and encouragement over the years.

Preface

THIS book had its beginning over twelve years ago when Jack Moore gave me my first tying instructions and a shoebox of tying material. I couldn't have been more than fourteen at the time but I began to tie in earnest, copying every fly pattern I could find. I began to visit various trout haunts, and I devoted most of my summers to fishing and backpacking. I supported this insatiable habit by tying lots of flies and selling them wholesale.

Over the years I have been fortunate enough to wander over much of the west pursuing my favorite pastimes . . . fly fishing, backpacking and photography. Countless fabled trout streams and pristine alpine lakes have unfolded before my eyes and to me there can be no greater thrill than enticing a beautiful trout to my feathered offering.

Tying nymphs has always been my favorite pursuit at the vise. Although the nymph patterns in this book have taken years to assemble and design, a book such as this is never complete since there will always be new patterns emerging from the tying desk. I have tried to select the most common and useful patterns throughout the country today, and I hope that all tying fishermen will gain some useful trick, hint, idea or pattern from these pages.

I welcome any useful ideas, information or patterns. I can be reached at Streamborn Flies, P. O. Box 23032, Tigard, Oregon 97223.

Part I:

Nymphs, Tools and Materials

Nymph Introduction

NYMPH fishing is the deadliest method of taking fish with a fly yet devised. The current popularity of "nymphing" can do doubt be linked to the fact that nymph fishermen catch most of the fish most of the time. This is easily explained as nymphs comprise roughly 90% of a trout's diet. Should a trout not like the taste of nymphs it would soon die. An alert, inventive, and inquisitive tying fisherman will *catch* fish . . . . . and hopefully release them.

From the casual fly fisherman's point of view, a nymph is any form of aquatic life which is found in the magical depths of water. This has come to mean that larva, scuds, crustaceans, shrimp, and a host of other underwater creatures are all referred to as nymphs. From a scientific point of view this is incorrect.

The entomologist defines a nymph, larva, or pupa as simply a stage in the development of an insect. Fly fishermen who refer to a shrimp imitation as a "shrimp nymph" do so simply because it is an underwater food of the trout, not because they think it will change into a winged insect. Many in-depth studies have been published on this subject and it is hoped that the serious student of angling will become familiar with the many varied aspects of the sport.

Briefly, a nymph has a precarious and varied life style, often spending a year or more in its underwater domain only to "emerge" into a winged adult insect, mate and die, sometimes in a matter of hours. The "emergence," as it is called, occurs when the nymphal insects shed their protective underwater casings and struggle to the surface. In the interim they have formed wings which will enable them to fly and mate before dying. It is during this time that they are most susceptible to the hungry trout, as they are adrift in the current and without the protection of the weed and gravel beds along the bottom. Only the fragile ecosystem of a lake or stream keeps the trout from gorging the nymphs to extinction thereby setting the stage for their own demise.

Other nymphs, like the stoneflies, will crawl out of the water and attach themselves to streamside vegetation. Here they abandon their casings and take to the air. Some nymph species will emerge for a few hours every day for weeks, while other varieties will appear to a much lesser degree. Each species is predictable as to its emergence dates which vary slightly from year to year depending on water and weather conditions.

The tying of nymphs can be as simple or involved as one wishes to make it. The fly fishing entomologists can become very scientific and construct exact imitations to fit their own personal angling needs. The inventive tying fisherman will hopefully search out the common insect life in his area and come up with some original imitations. Many of the nymph patterns contained in this book closely resemble actual insects while others do not. At times unfortunately, the angler will be unable to relate the identity of the imitation to that of the natural. Many patterns, which have evolved over the years, are copies of certain insects but have taken on the name of the innovator and not that of the actual nymph it imitates.

A casual fisherman, therefore, will fish a Hare's Ear with consistent success but not fully understand why. Does it closely resemble a resident insect or is it an attractor or "simulator" pattern? Close scrutiny of the stream's life should reveal the secret. Simulator patterns are often fished with phenomenal success, despite the puzzling fact that they apparently have no resemblance to anything living or dead at least not to the casual eye of the fisherman. Many nymphs are tied simply to suggest forms of aquatic life rather than to actually duplicate them. Often times a fish has to decide in a split second if what it sees is a tasty tidbit or a fraud. In situations like this a real life-like imitation is generally not necessary and the fisherman can often fish a suggestive pattern over a wide range of conditions and do quite well.

Probably the most important ingredients in a simulator pattern are size and color. At other times, especially during low water conditions and in slow-slick pools, eddies and lakes, the fish has plenty of time to make a leisurely inspection of the offering before accepting or rejecting it. In such situations the fish will often be extremely selective, and nothing but a life-like offering presented in a natural manner will bring a strike.

Collecting Nymphs

THE interested student of fly fishing will want to collect aquatic insects from the water he fishes for identification and a close up view of what his imitation should look like to fool selective fish. The would-be collector will need a net or screen to trap the nymphs. A nylon net dries fast, is strong and easily carried. Wire mesh nets are handy for faster water where you want to cover a larger area of stream, but this type net is bulky and doesn't fold up for placemet into a vest pocket.

Ideal mesh is 24-32 strands per inch. Stretch the screen across the current. If you have a cohort send him immediately upstream of the net to lift up a couple rocks and make a general disturbance. Do not desecrate the area, simply dislodge a few insects. These will drift into the net for easy observation. A small strainer is useful for dipping insects out of lake or pond.

Look for nymphs along the bottom of lakes, in weed beds, gravel, sand, in aquatic vegetation and on or under stones. Leaves gathered from the streambed and laid out to dry will reveal a host of crawling insects. For those interested in more specific collecting methods and in exact identification pick up a copy of *"Aquatic Insects of California,"* by R. Usinger. This 500 page reference volumn is indispensable and covers nearly all aquatic insects found in North America.

Mayflies

OF ALL the aquatic life the mayflies have fluttered in the forefront of angling literature for 500 years. Angling readers have been deluged with mayfly nymphs, emergers, duns and spinners. These beautifully fragile, veined-winged insects are the inspiration for most of the feathered dry flies and nymphs in our treasured angling boxes. It is only recently that the angling masses have become aware of the other equally important insects which trout feed upon.

Mayflies are very prolific and are forage food for countless animals. Size and coloration are endless, though many nymphs take on a brownish hue. Sizes commonly range from 10—24 with some larger and smaller ones also present. Mayfly nymphs primarily have articulated gills along the sides of the body, three hairy tail fibers and a thorax about one-third the overall length of the body. Adults will have two to three long, delicate tails, upright veined wings and

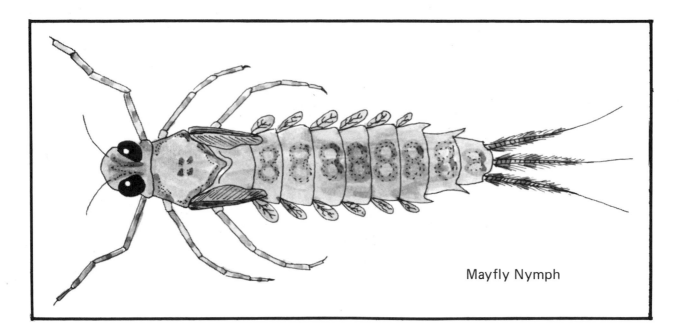

Mayfly Nymph

a curve to their body. Both nymphs and adults are very fragile.

Look for mayfly nymphs along the bottom of lakes and ponds. Check gravel, sand and weed beds in streams. Depending on the type, mayfly nymphs are either crawlers, burrowers, free swimmers or clingers. Mayfly life cycles range from a few months to two years. A few species emerge by crawling out of the water onto dry rocks or vegetation where they shed their nymphal case along the back, climb out, dry their wings and fly off to the protection of nearby bushes. Adults live only a few hours to a maximum of a few days.

Mayflies hatch just about every month of the year depending on water and air temperature. Small, isolated winter time hatches are generally confined to warmer spring creeks on suitable days but it is not unusual to witness a good hatch on a snowy afternoon in early spring. Generally speaking the sporadic hatches of winter do not compare to the clouds of mayflies which send trout into a feeding frenzie throughout the summer months.

Stoneflies

M OST fishermen will quickly become familiar with the stoneflies, especially the larger species found throughout the West. Many of these nymphs attain a length of two inches and are often referred to as salmon flies or helgramites. In many of the larger and faster waters of the West these insects are the first or second most important food for trout. Streams with an unusally large population of stonefly nymphs often produce many large trout. Appalachian and Great Lakes area streams also support fine populations of stoneflies but they seldom exceed an inch in length and usually range from one to three quarters inches in length. Hatches are often sporadic but stoneflies never-the-less provide many meals for the trout. Size and coloration are nearly endless as there are between 400 and 500 species found in North America.

With few exceptions, stoneflies require running water with lots of oxygen to propagate and consequently are usually only found in streams. The most prolific hatches occur in spring and early summer, but scattered hatches can be found every month of the year in some sections of the country. The most publicized hatches are the salmon fly and golden stone, but many stoneflies hatch in oranges, yellows, browns, greens and black.

Stoneflies feed on vegetation and other aquatic life. Streams which have large populations of stoneflies will usually have meager populations of mayfly nymphs, due to the stonefly pre-

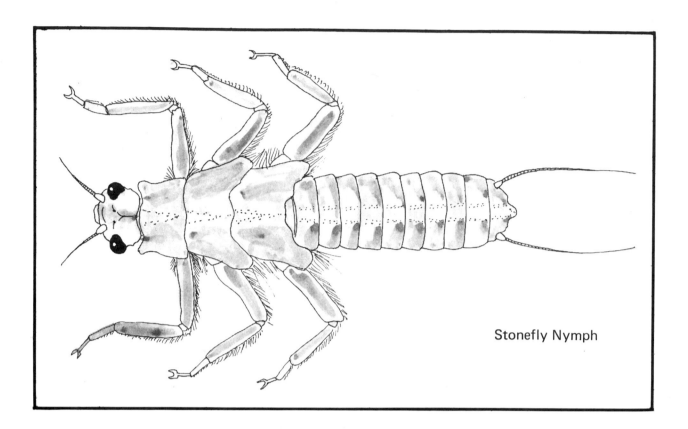

Stonefly Nymph

dation. Stonefly nymphs can be easily identified by the three seperate sections of the thorax, its overall length being equal to the body. Bodies have 10 segments and a short forked tail. Gills are sometimes located under the thorax area, but never along the sides of the body as is the case with mayfly nymphs. The life cycle is usually a year, but some have a two or three year cycle. Nymphs emerge from their underwater domain by crawling out of the stream and attaching themselves to streamside vegetation. Once there they shed their protective casing and take to the air as winged adults.

Caddis

ROUGHLY 100 species of caddis flies have been identified in North America. Angling history has all but forgotten the secretive caddis fly, which has recently come to be more important to many anglers than the storied mayflies.

Some nymphs, or larvae, swim free in the current, while others spin nets like a spider for protection and the gathering of food. Others build cases of twigs, sand, pebbles and leaves. The durability of the case will often depend on the water current, with some lake species hardly having a case at all. Many species live completely exposed on sand or gravel, while others attach themselves to rocks or weeds.

Colors generally span the yellows, browns, greens and black, with a tan colored nymph being very abundant. Sizes are mostly 8-14 but some are larger. Adult caddis flies (often called sedges) have two antennae, and are easily recognized by the mottled brown wing which is folded back over the top of the body in a "V." These wary insects seldom fly actively until dark. During the day the caddis will seek shelter in damp, dark places.

I have witnessed a big green caddis, hatching in the mountains of the far west well after dark, sending the trout to the surface in star light. Caddis are well scattered throughout North America but prefer cool, clean water. Hatches can be found nearly any given month, but the main hatches occur in the summer. I have seen clouds of these descend on spring creeks and mountain lakes driving the fish crazy.

10

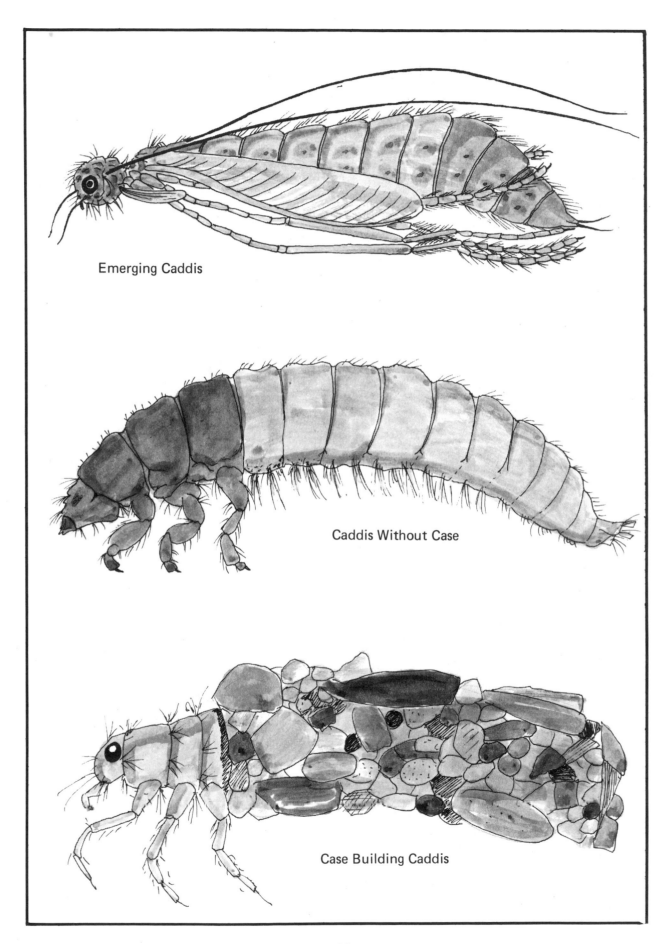

Emerging Caddis

Caddis Without Case

Case Building Caddis

Dragon and Damsel Flies

DAMSEL or dragon flies are known by many names, two of the more common being the mosquito hawk and devil fly. Dragon flies are very attractive with many adults being blue or red. They are very strong fliers, and can be found around nearly all bodies of water. Despite their menacing appearance they are quite useful and do not harm man. A few of the larger species can inflict a harmless bite, but they represent no threat.

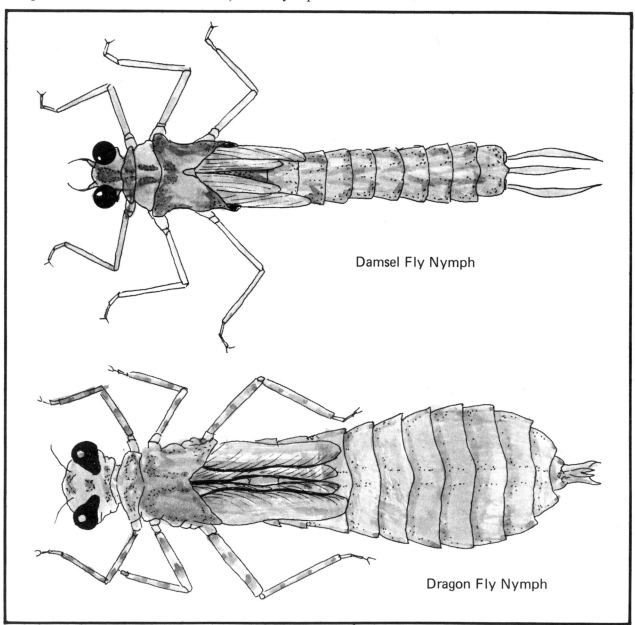

Damsel Fly Nymph

Dragon Fly Nymph

The nymphs, many of them being highly cannibalistic, are often two inches or longer in length, and are highly prized by the fish. The dark browns and greens are the best known to fishermen.

After a year or so the nymphs crawl out of the water, attach themselves to nearby vegetation, and hatch into winged adults. Winged adults often have over a 5" wing span. Dragon fly nymphs differ from damsel fly nymphs in that they are much thicker and heavier in appearance and should be tied accordingly. The angler's fly selection would be incomplete without a selection of these abundant insects.

Freshwater Shrimp and Scuds

F reshwater shrimp and scuds are often confused by fishermen. Both belong to the class Crustacea and are difficult to tell apart by the casual observer. Shrimp are very similar in appearance to their saltwater cousins and are generally larger than scuds. Scuds will seldom attain lengths of over an inch, averaging three-quarters of an inch in length. The very nature of scud bodies suggest a curved or humped appearance to the observer. However scuds generally swim with their bodies completely outstretched and imitations should be tied accordingly. Scuds are more abundant than shrimp and they play an important role in the angling efforts of knowledgeable fishermen.

Many of the more famous waters across North America are inhabited by these high protein creatures. Spring creeks in the Yellowstone area, Pennsylvania, the Sierras, and the Cascades often contain huge populations of scuds. Many lakes throughout the country harbor astronomical numbers of scuds. In such waters trout often gain over two pounds per year! Lakes with enormous populations of scuds include Yellowstone Lake, Henrys Lake, most lakes throughout the western desert region and some alpine lakes. I have found excellent populations of both scuds and trout in lakes over 12,000 feet. The best time to observe these unique creatures is early and late in the day when shadows are present. Look for them around shoreline vegetation, especially in weedy areas.

Most scud or shrimp imitations available in sport shops are poor imitations at best. The ever present, widely curved "pink shrimp" is not nearly as effective as you might expect. This dressing probably came into existence by some tier observing shrimp neatly packaged

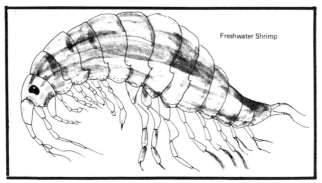

Freshwater Shrimp

at the local meat counter. Scuds and shrimp do have a tendency to turn a slightly pinkish tan in color when dead or when molting, but I have never seen a bright "pink" shrimp. The most common colors are tan, gray, brown, olive and combinations thereof, with gray-olive and gray-brown being two of the most common combinations.

Tools

G OOD tools are to a fly tier what balanced tackle is to a fly fisherman. While it is quite possible to tie a fly with little more aid than ones hands, for the maximum enjoyment of this pursuit it is essential to obtain good tools. Proper tools will last for years, and you won't have to worry about repairing them. After experimenting with nearly all available tools for over ten years, I have settled on the following. These are the most practical for beginner or professional.

Vise: The qualities to look for in a vise are durability, and the ability to hold a wide range of hook sizes securely. Nothing is more frustrating than a constantly slipping hook in the vise.

There is little debate among professional tyers that the Thompson A is the accepted standard. It is simple and fast to operate and can be adjusted for height. The Thompson B is also good, but it lacks the fast lever action clamp and does not adjust for height.

Crest Tool manufactures two good vises. These are the Crest and the Supreme, both of which are becoming quite popular. For a finely machined, durable vise, which is capable of many adjustments, and also of holding just about any size hook, I would recommend the Salmo Vise. This is a European import.

Bobbin: No other tool causes more controversy than the bobbin. Some tiers feel it is bothersome, or that it produces an inferior quality fly. I originally learned without a bobbin, and later began using one, so I have seen both sides of the stream, so to speak. In my opinion, anyone who ties without a bobbin is doing himself a disservice. I wouldn't instruct anyone without a bobbin. Besides being like a third hand, a bobbin can double your speed. There are a lot of worthless bobbins on the market, and I don't recommend using just any brand.

The only two I can recommend are the Frank Matarelli and the Crest Custom. Frank Matarelli first came out with his clip type in the 1950's. The Matarelli is entirely stainless steel, making it lighter and more durable than the Crest. The Matarelli will not fray or cut your thread. Both bobbins are easily adjustable for tension, and should be readily available at any specialty shop tuned in to the latest methods.

Scissors: Most any scissors will do in a pinch, but sharp, fine point scissors are a joy to use. I prefer scissors with large finger holes, that can be carried on the hand while tying. While the scissors I use are made in Italy, Crest Tool is distributing lance-like shears that are extremely sharp, easy to carry in your hand and excellent for cutting fur. Curved scissors are popular for trimming hair bodies and for cutting in tight areas. Check around and find a pair that feel comfortable to you. Features to keep in mind are durability, sharpness, a fine point and large finger holes.

Hackle Pliers: There is an abundance of hackle pliers on the market. The English are making a good lightweight model that comes in three sizes. These pliers have a piece of rubber on one side and they will slip off the feather before breaking it. Crest tool also has a good pair, as does Danville. The Danville pliers are by far the most rigid and sure gripping, but they will break the feather before slipping off if one isn't careful.

The best pliers I have found are my fingers. They are fast, easy to work with and they don't slip . . . at least not yet. I only reach for the pliers when tying midges. Regardless, most tiers find pliers an excellent aid, and professionals keep them around for special needs, so these would be a wise investment.

Whipfinisher: A useful tool for some people, though I find one unnecessary. I would suggest the Thompson or smaller Martarelli tools. Instructions are provided with the tool.

Material Clip: This is an inexpensive clip that fits most any vise, and keeps threads, tinsels, etc., held back out of your way while tying. I wouldn't be without this attachment.

Lamp: Find a good lamp. Don't subject your eyes to tying by a dim light. Look for a high intensity lamp that will throw out a concentrated beam but will not heat up. You should keep in mind the lightweight spring action type that can easily be slipped into a suitcase for those away from home tying and fishing adventures.

Croydon Hand Vise: A small, simple tool, designed to allow the fly tier to tie along the stream or just about anywhere. This vise easily holds hooks from size 10-28.

Bodkin: Whether it be for scouring or picking out a dubbed body, applying lacquer to

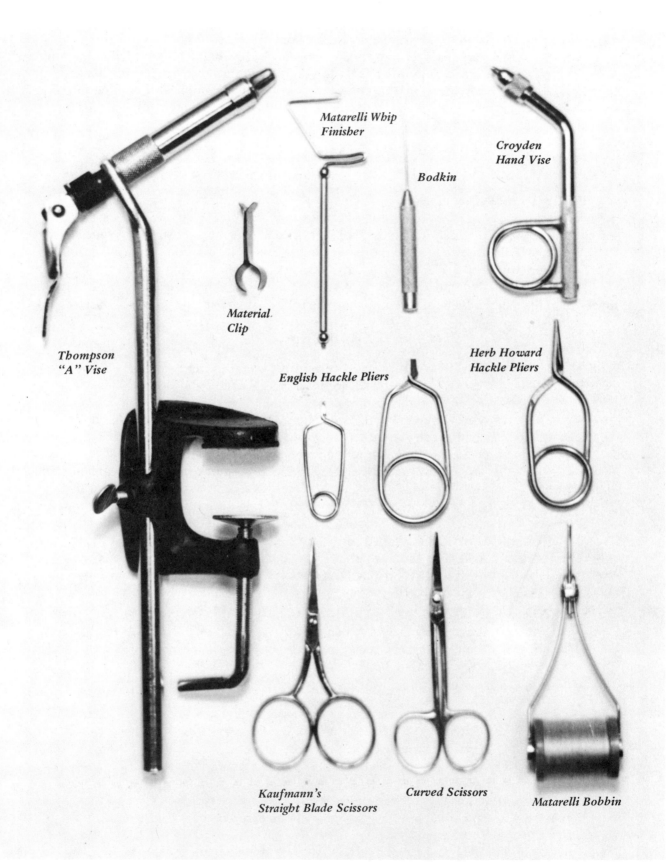

Matarelli Whip
Finisher

Croyden
Hand Vise

Bodkin

Material
Clip

Thompson
"A" Vise

Herb Howard
Hackle Pliers

English Hackle Pliers

Kaufmann's
Straight Blade Scissors

Curved Scissors

Matarelli Bobbin

a fly, or just poking around, this inexpensive tool should be on your bench.

    Glue Bottle: A very handy set up for applying glue (providing you don't have children around) is to attach a standard bottle of glue to your vise with rubber bands. Punch a nail hole in the cap and insert a bodkin. You now have an instant glue applicator with no more spillage or cap unscrewing. Naturally, you will have to add a little thinner from time to time.

Hooks

THE fly tier often is confronted by such an array of hooks that he is usually at a loss as to which purchase would be best. Mustad carries an incredible selection of hooks and are recognized as one of the best, with most shops stocking a wide range of sizes and types. Eagle Claw-Wright McGill also produces a fine quality hook, but their selection is somewhat limited.

    Nymph tiers will need a selection of 1X to 4X shank hooks in assorted sizes in their kit, along with a few standard lengths. The 1X designation means the hook shank is one eye length longer than the standard length. I recommend the following, depending on which patterns you wish to tie.

MUSTAD:

3906 size 8-14	This is basically a standard wet fly hook, but can be used for nymphs.
3906B size 8-16	The "B" denotes a 1X long shank as per the 3906 variety. This is a very useful nymph hook.
9671 size 2-14	A good nymph hook for medium size flies, the 9671 is also used for small streamers and wooly worms, 9671 is 2X long.
9672 size 2-14	One of the more popular nymph hooks, the 9672 is a 3X long shank as per the 9671. This is also a good long wooly worm, medium streamer and muddler hook.
79580 size 2-14	A hook like the 9672 only 4X long. It lends itself nicely to extra long stoneflies, and is useful for many streamers and flies where an extra long hook shank is called for.
38941 size 2-12	A 3X long, hollow point, sproat hook used for some western type nymphs.
7957BX size 2-16	A 1X long, 1X strong, heavy hook which is becoming extremely popular with nymph tiers.
9575 size 2-12	A 6X long loop eye limerick hook which we now prefer for stone flies, dragons, damsels, streamers, etc. Has a narrow bite, which greatly reduces the chance of hooking fish in the eye. We no longer encourage the use of the Eagle Claw 1206.

Hook Plate

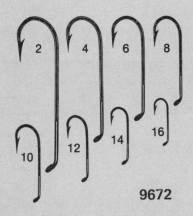

9672

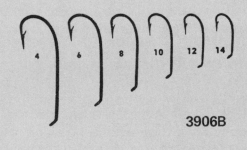

3906B

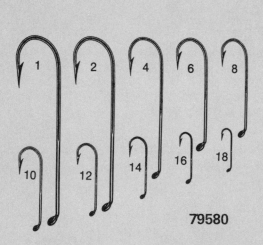

79580

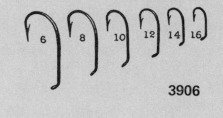

3906

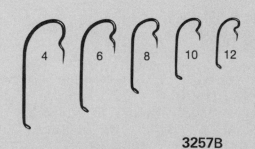

3257B

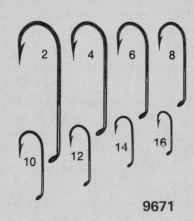

9671

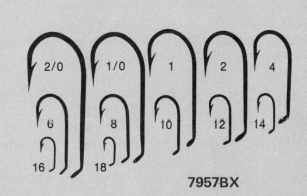

7957BX

Materials

MATERIALS can be very confusing, especially for the beginning tier. The following list will serve as a guide for the beginning nymph tier, and can also help the advanced tier to effectively build up his material kit. Even though it may cost a little more, be certain to obtain the best quality possible when purchasing your material. No one can tie a quality fly with inferior quality materials.

Neck Hackle: "Hackle" is the feather from the neck of a gamecock rooster. It is commonly purchased, on the skin, as a "neck." Saddle hackles are the long hackles which drape down the sides of a rooster and these are also quite useful. The difference between a neck and saddle hackle is mainly in the length and width of the feather. Saddle hackles are much longer and generally wider than neck hackles. This means that saddle hackles are only suitable for larger flies. Primarily hook sizes 2-10; while neck hackles are best suited for the smaller nymphs in sizes 8-22. Besides being used for standard hackling, these feathers are commonly utilized for tails, legs and feelers.

When purchasing a neck, look for one with a wide range of hackle sizes. A good neck will have lots of smaller hackles. The nymph tier doesn't need a dry fly quality neck, but don't buy a small skimpy neck with wide, limp hackle either. Saddle hackle comes bundled or strung on a string. *Never* buy loose hackles. Besides being difficult to sort, they are mostly junk and generally a poor buy. Neck hackles should be purchased in the following colors: brown, cream, furnace, black, olive, blue dun and grizzly. Saddle hackles should be stocked in browns, grizzly and black.

HACKLE COLOR EXPLANATION:

NATURAL DARK BLUE DUN:	Dark grayish to a smoky black. Very rare. A true natural dun color is quite different from the blue dun capes offered on the market. They are often very dark and don't "lighten up" until tied and exposed to full sunlight.
DARK GINGER:	Pale brown or golden brown.
COACHMAN BROWN:	A dark chocolate shade used for Royal Coachman patterns.
FURNACE:	Brown feathers with a black center as in a badger.
BADGER:	Black center with white to golden tips.
CREAM:	Pale ginger to an off-white.
CREE:	Brown varigated with black bars.
NATURAL GINGER:	True ginger shade, lighter than a dark ginger.
HONEY DUN:	A subtle gingerish two-tone color.
GINGER VARIANT:	Ginger color overall, but with some light and dark barring.
FIERY VARIANT:	Rich brown with lighter barring.
LIGHT VARIANT:	Light cream cast with ginger to brown mottling. Looks cream in color when tied with shaded effect. All variants add a natural color effect to a fly.
GRIZZLY:	Definite black and white barring.
IMITATION GRIZZLY:	A light base with nearly black barring. Mixes well with solid colors or use as is. Rare.
NAIROBI:	Two tone necks, that is necks containing two separate colored hackles, such as white and brown.
DYED BLUE DUN:	Light, medium and dark. These are greyish blue and the standard dun color.

Threads

THE nymph tier will want to obtain about a half dozen different colors of thread. It is often advisable to use a color of thread that compliments the over all color of the fly. The most practical thread to use on nymphs is pre-wax nylon in size 6/0. This is very strong for its size and the tacky wax lends itself nicely to dubbing. Pre-wax is also available in 3/0. This is marketed under the Danville label. Do not accept substitutes. The nylon thread being manufactured today is far superior to silk as it handles quite easily and is very strong. Best colors are black, brown, olive, yellow and gray.

Hair

THE nymph tier will find very little use for hair. With the exception of a few special ties, the only need for hair will be for some tails. A selection of two or three shades of deer hair, moose body hair and a red and gray squirrel tail should be sufficient.

Fur

THE nymph tier can never have enough fur. Fur bodied nymphs are exceptionally popular with both the fisherman *and* the fish. Fur bodied flies project such an uncanny likeness when wet, they will often fool fish when other materials are rejected.

Some of the new yarns on the market are also quite good, but natural fur has the advantage. Beaver, muskrat, otter, hare's ear, seal and rabbit will prove the most useful. There are other suitable furs but these are the most important.

Rabbit should be purchased in at least 10 natural and dyed colors. It dubs on nicely and a wide selection of colors are readily available. When the tier wants that special color during a late night tying session he will have it.

Seal is my favorite material as it lends itself nicely to dubbing and makes for a buggy, translucent body that drives fish crazy. In the past seal was readily available, but today, due to import restrictions, it is becoming quite scarce. If you can find some genuine seal, buy it and use it. If you cannot find genuine seal, settle on one of the several available substitutes.

Seal also mixes well with other furs and several patterns call for seal mixed with otter, rabbit or muskrat. If you mix black seal with black rabbit the resulting effect is a smooth underbody with many buggy guard hairs protruding to give the fly excellent breathing action and a true translucent appearance. The possibilities here are unlimited. Rabbit and seal fur is best obtained in browns, yellows, black, cream, grays and greens.

For the tying and ribbing of bodies a few more materials are necessary. Purchase rayon floss, preferably four strand. The tier can use all four or a single strand, depending on the size fly to be tied. Chenille, while not particularily buggy looking, is called for in several patterns. Pick out a selection of natural colors in small and medium sizes. The best colors are black, browns, yellows and greens.

Yarn

MOHLON is without a doubt the best synthetic yarn on the market. It is very easy to tie with and comes in a fine selection of natural colors, of which the greens, grays browns, yellows and black are the most popular. When wet, mohlon attracts lots of air bubbles and has a good deal more life than regular yarn. I prefer it over the polyester yarn. Polyester yarn is very popular, however, and can be cut up and blended into many fine colors. It comes in yarn and sheet form with about 15 colors being available.

Tinsel

TINSELS are very useful and no tier can get along without them. A selection of gold and silver in flat and oval should be on your tying bench. Stock up with medium and small sizes for large tinsel is seldom needed. Fine wire is perhaps the most useful ribbing material of all. Besides being used for ribbing it is an excellent reinforcer on fragile bodies such as peacock and floss. It is also excellent for adding a slight amount of flash and for depicting a segmented effect. Gold, silver and copper are the most useful colors.

Miscellaneous Materials

THE following materials will prove indispensable for the tying of tails, legs, wings, wing-cases and hackles. An assortment of colors should be on hand.

Mallard flank feathers in natural gray, dyed wood duck color and gold. (Olive, yellow and blue dun are also useful.)

Stripped goose is a must in white, black, green, blue, brown, gray, olive and gold. Stripped goose is excellent for wingcases whenever these colors are called for. Many popular patterns call for it on tails, wings and antennae, and it is extremely easy to tie with, and is very realistic and durable.

Turkey quills in natural brown are a must. Several dyed colors are also useful. Partridge hackles in grey and brown are nearly indispensable. Ostrich in gray, browns and black will come in handy, and other colors may be added as the need arises. Peacock herl is extremely popular and should be bought on string, swords and choice eyed tail feathers.

Ringneck pheasant rump feathers and tail fibers are useful, and a complete skin will also come in handy for those rare-colored feathers on special ties. Lead wire is a must and you should stock small, medium and large. About the last thing you will need, besides some trout water, is fly head cement, clear lacquer or varnish. When applied to the head, your knot will be secure and your flies should last until you loose them.

The preceding selection will prove most useful. Other items will be needed from time to time but this is an excellent start and will enable you to tie most of the flies listed in this book.

Parts of a Tied Nymph

Tail: The purpose of the tail on the nymph is for stability and natural appearance. For the most part tails should be short, sparse and unobtrusive. Nearly any material can be used for tails. Most popular materials are mallard flank, gamecock hackle, partridge and stripped goose.

Many of the more recent nymphs tied with stripped goose are tied in the shape of a "V." The fibers are tied in such a manner that they flare away from each other. Fibers should be mounted along the sides of the hook so they appear to come out of the side of the body.

Ribbing: Ribbing is referred to as any material (other than hackle) which is wrapped around the body and evenly spaced. The basic idea behind the rib is to "set off" the body, add a slight amount of flash, act as a reinforcer and to depict segmentation. It is important not to overdo the ribbing because it is meant to be a subtle part of a nymph. Ribbing should be evenly spaced and tightly wrapped. Tinsel is most often used for ribbing but thread, peacock and ostrich are also commonly used. Oval and flat tinsels are most commonly used in small sizes as is fine wire.

Body: The body on a nymph is very important. It should nearly always have a taper to it with the taper building up toward the front of the fly. Many nymph bodies are two part, in which case the actual body should be slightly over half the length of the hook shank. Keep in mind that the body and thorax should be almost evenly divided with the body being slightly longer on many occasions, depending on the nymph pattern.

Hackle: There are several types of hackle with which you should be familiar. All hackle, except palmered hackle, is tied in at the front of the fly, usually just behind the eye of the hook. When the term "hackle" is used it refers to a complete hackle that encircles the entire front of the fly. The most common material is rooster neck hackle, but hackles on some patterns call for partridge or mallard feathers.

On nymphs and wet flies hackles are "tied back." This means that after the fibers have been secured they are swept back along the body of the fly and secured in that position with the thread. Palmered hackle, as with most hackle, represents legs and moving body parts and lends a buggy look to the imitation. Palmering the hackle is simply the winding of hackle through the body or thorax in much the same way you would wind ribbing. Palmered hackle is usually tied in the same way as regular hackle but sometimes for special effect it is tied in tip first.

Beard hackle denotes that a small bunch of feather fibers are tied in at the head area along the underside of the hook (bottom of fly). Beard hackle should extend to about the point of the hook but not beyond. Beard hackle is sometimes tied in behind the thorax to represent legs on special ties.

Head: This term will refer to the area immediately behind the actual thread head. Heads are often confused with the thorax, but are actually much smaller and a fly pattern may call for both a thorax and a head. A good example of this is the Giant Black nymph. Heads generally represent both fuzzy heads and small legs, and are most often tied with ostrich or peacock herl.

Antennae: This is a fiber or two which protrudes from the head of the nymph and represents the actual antennae or feelers of a natural insect.

Thorax: Another very important part of the nymph is the thorax. The thorax basically is a continuation of the nymph body, but it is usually a good deal larger in diameter and often constructed of a different material or color than the body. The thorax is mainly representative of the forward half of the insect.

Collar: The collar is usually a bunch of fur or feather tied in front of the thorax in such a manner that it extends around the thorax.

Shellback: This is a piece of material tied in at the tail, on top of the hook, and pulled forward over the top of the body and tied off at the head. The shellback is popular in many shrimp imitations.

Wingcase: The wingcase seems to put the finishing touch on a nymph — at least to the eyes of the fisherman. It is a section of feather which is tied in on top of the hook before beginning the thorax. After the thorax has been completed the wingcase material is pulled over

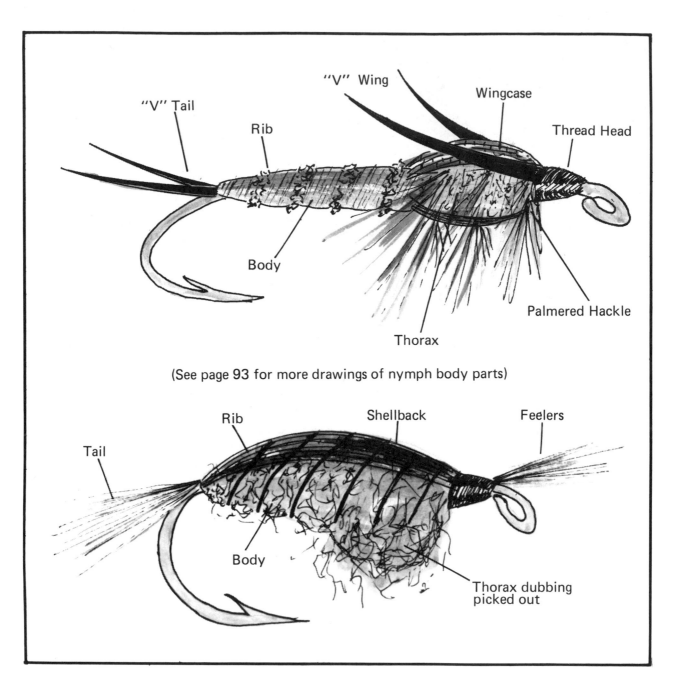

"V" Tail

"V" Wing

Wingcase

Thread Head

Rib

Body

Palmered Hackle

Thorax

(See page 93 for more drawings of nymph body parts)

Rib

Shellback

Feelers

Tail

Body

Thorax dubbing picked out

the top of the thorax and tied off at the head. This represents the wing pad area of the actual nymph where the wings will grow as the nymph matures into an adult insect. Common materials are stripped goose, turkey quill and duck wing quill.

Wings: Wings are very similar to the wingcase but this is often one of the last steps in the tying of a nymph. The wings usually represent a more advanced life stage than the wingcase. The wings are simply tied on top of the hook over the top of the thorax and are often clipped to size. Two stripped goose fibers are often used for wings. These are tied in the shape of a "V" over the top of the body area, and then spread out at an angle so that the tips flare up.

Thread Head: The thread head is where the tier finishes off the fly with a knot, after which he applies a generous amount of lacquer. Heads should be neat and smooth in appearance with a slight taper. The beginning tier tends to crowd the head and doesn't leave enough room to finish off the fly. A small space should be left bare of all wrappings where the final head will go. This will insure enough room.

Blending Furs

F UR blending seemed to be invented especially for the nymph tier. This simple method allows the tier to create unlimited colors and textured effects. All that is needed is a blender, warm water, soap and a strainer. Clip the desired fur, polly yarn, seal or other choice into a small pile making sure the fur isn't lumpy or unduly matted. Some furs may have to be picked apart before they are blended. This will allow a more thorough mixing in the blender.

Clip yarns in one inch strips and unravel. Experiment a bit because the possibilities are limited only by your imagination. Place the fur to be mixed in a blender along with warm water and a drop or two of liquid detergent. Mix a minute or two until the fur is well blended. Then remove it, rinse through a strainer, squeeze out the excess water and dry. This is referred to as matted fur.

Dubbing

N OTHING in the art of fly tying, unless it would be the mounting of quill wings, seems to be more mystical than dubbing. For the novice dubbing is the method of applying loose fur directly to the tying thread in such a manner that it becomes a thread-like strand itself.

While there are many dubbing methods in use today, the simplest I have found is to pull out some fur and spread it evenly and *thinly* along prewax thread between your thumb and first two fingers. Then roll the fur onto the thread, *always* rolling the fur in the same direction, applying lots of pressure between your thumb and forefinger. *Do not* roll it back and forth as this will cause the fur to bunch up and wrap around the thread in a bulky, uneven manner. With a little practice a nice, tight, evenly tapered body will be a cinch and dubbing will become quicker than working with yarn.

Dubbing pure seal is a little more difficult. Seal is coarse and does not adhere to the thread

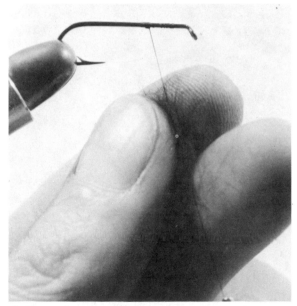

1. Spread out a small amount of fur along a section of thread

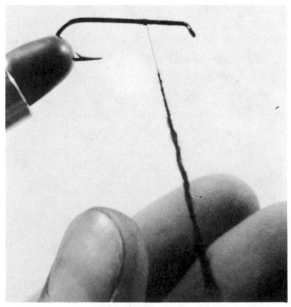

2. Using your thumb and two fingers roll the fur onto the thread applying lots of pressure, remember, always roll in the same direction — do not roll back and forth

like soft fur. Do a *little* at a time. Do not try to roll it onto the thread very tight as this will prove futile. Roll it very loosely and wrap it onto the hook. Repeat this process as many times as is necessary. You may have to go over the body two times. Many tiers like to mix seal fur with a little smooth fur so it rolls tighter. One may also dub seal over fur. To do this, dub the fur onto the thread and then apply seal over the fur before wrapping it onto the hook.

Twisting

TWISTING is the method of wrapping a tight segmented body with any type of yarn or fur. Mohlon is ideally adapted to this method and bodies tied in this manner are very durable and realistic looking. Twisting is done by cutting a suitable length of mohlon and tying it onto the underside of the hook. Then pulling the thread down alongside the mohlon, t take the thread and mohlon in hand and spin the two together until both are tightly wrapped around each other. When wrapping the two together it is important to do the spinning at the end of the mohlon, not in the middle. Next, hold the two tightly together at the extreme end and begin to wrap the body being careful not to let them unwind. Notice the segmented look this creates. I have put this method to use on many standard patterns and the resulting effect is excellent. By slightly building up the underbody a perfect taper is easily mastered.

The same effect is accomplished with fur by tying it in tip first and spreading it down along the thread while rolling it between your thumb and first two fingers. It is important not to let the fur and thread unwind. Keep tension the entire time. (Twisting fur on Page 26)

TWISTING MOHLON:

1: Build up a taperd underbody if desired and mount mohlon on the underside of the hook, this will allow it to fall in line with the thread

2: Secure the mohlon at the extreme rear of the hook and pull it down along the thread

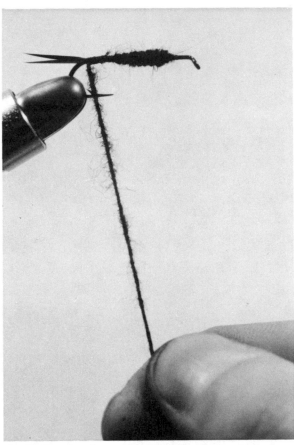
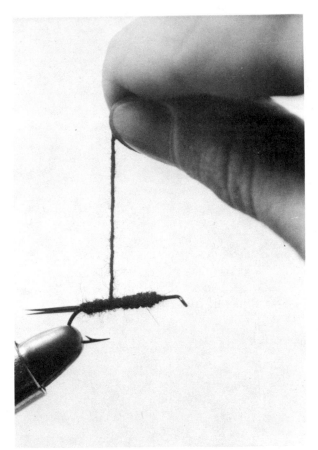

3: Twist the thread and mohlon together, when twisting be certain to grab the thread and mohlon at the extreme end, this will keep the mohlon from becoming soiled and matted, and you will easily be able to tell when it is twisted as tight as possible

4: Be extremely careful not to let the two unravel while winding on the body

5: Close up view of twisted mohlon body depicting segmentation

TWISTING FUR:

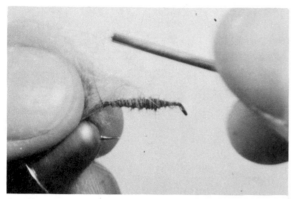

1: Tie in a good sized clump of fur tip first, don't try to tie in all the tips, just the longer fibers of fur

2: Proper way to tie in the fur tips

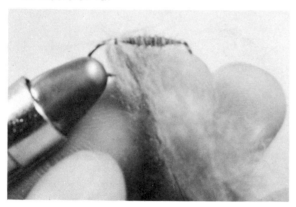

3: Begin rolling the fur over your two fingers catching the thread core with your thumb

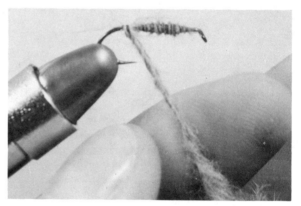

4: Repeat the process and slowly work the fur down the thread as you roll the fur tight, don't let up on the tension

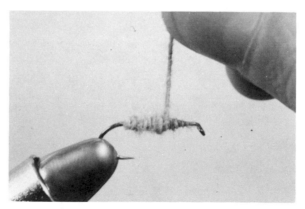

5: When all of the fur is tightly rolled onto the thread grip the end and proceed to wrap the body, if properly done and tightly wrapped, the body should have definite segments like this

Underbodies

MOST flies should have a slight taper to the body. When constructing smaller flies a slight taper is easily mastered by beginning the body material in the center of the body and wrapping forward first, then all the way back and forward again. With many larger flies this would take an endless quantity of fur so some heavy material like mohlon or floss is used first to build up a taper. Floss can be rapidly applied by using a stainless steel bobbin.

An underbody is especially advisable when tying with peacock as it has little body to it. Peacock is very thin so two to five herls should usually be wrapped at once. This, coupled with an underbody, is the best way to achieve a fat, juicy body.

A Word About Peacock

1: Peacock body without underbody

2: Tapered fur underbody before winding two strands of peacock

3: Finished peacock body when wrapped over tapered underbody

PEACOCK is used very extensively in the tying of flies because it has a beautiful natural color and appearance. A "juicy" body is often desired and this is easily done by building up an underbody and using two or more pieces of peacock.

Peacock herl may be "stripped" by soaking it in a 50-50 solution of bleach and water for a minute or two and agitating it and then stripping the herl off with your fingers. Rinse well

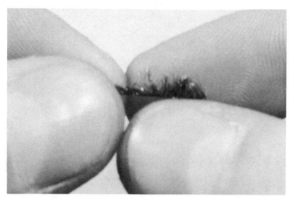

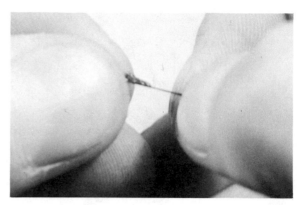

1: Using thumb and forefinger to strip   2: Peeling off peacock quill

and place the stripped peacock in some fabric softener for a short time. This method will often fade the herl slightly and if you're not careful the peacock quill will become quite brittle due to too much bleach. Be sure to wear rubber gloves and old clothing when doing this.

Another, but slower, method is to strip the herl off the quill with your thumb and forefinger as can be seen in the photographs. Peacock herl is quite fragile so be careful not to exert too much pressure. This method makes a fine soft quill but it is time consuming for professional tiers. Peacock herl may also be removed with an eraser. It is advisable to rib peacock bodies with fine wire, since this will make them much more durable.

Lead Wire Weighted Flies

LEAD wire is one of the most important aids a nymph tier can employ. The wire is used to add extra weight to a fly which allows it to sink rapidly and reach the desired depth below the surface. A fly should be weighted to the degree of depth you wish to fish. Naturally, the more wire the faster and deeper the nymph will sink. There is a definite advantage in tying your own flies, since all commercial flies are uniformly weighted and not tailored to individual needs. Lead wire is generally sold in three sizes: small, medium and large. The diameter will range from .015 to .035 and all sizes are indispensable. A half pound of wire is still your best buy and it can be divided between yourself and your tying friends.

When applying lead wire it is best to do so over a thread base because it creates a rough surface for the smooth wire to bite into. Wrap your thread over and through the wire to be certain it's secure and won't roll around the hook shank. For a flattened effect take smooth nosed pliers and gently squeeze the wire until it's flat. Then apply a generous amount of glue and proceed to tie the fly. Flatten the body upon completion and before the glue has set up.

Lead wire should be mounted on the front three quarters of the hook shank, leaving a space one quarter inch or so at the front of the shank so a neat tapered head can be formed. By starting the wire at the front of the hook shank a nice tapered body can be constructed and there will be ample room at the rear to tie in the tail, ribbing and body material.

Many patterns in this book are listed as weighted. The weighted designation has been placed on those patterns which are generally tied in that manner but wire may be added or omitted from any pattern. This is left completely to the discretion of the tier.

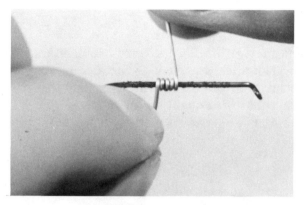

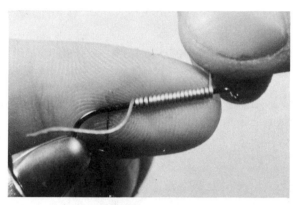

1: Wind a covering of thread to give the wire a rough surface, now begin to wrap the wire very tightly and close together

2: By holding your left forefinger on the wire and pulling the end with your right fingers the wire will break off very close, this will prevent jagged ends and dull scissors

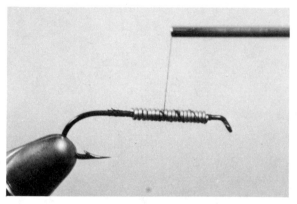

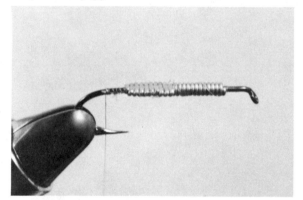

3: Secure with several wraps of thread

4: By compressing the wire with flat nosed pliers, a nice flattened effect is easily mastered, be careful not to compress the wire too tight or it will crumble

Substitutions

A TIER will often run across a pattern calling for a foreign material. While it is advisable to follow a pattern as closely as possible, many times another material will cause little if any change in the appearance .

A classic example of this is the lemon wood duck feather. When properly dyed a mallard flank feather comes extremely close in color and texture. As a tier becomes familiar with the various furs and feathers he will recognize the differences and similarities, and near perfect substitutions will become almost automatic.

One of the more common substitutions would be stripped goose for condor. The magnificent condor is an endangered species. Goose, besides being readily available and reasonable, is better suited for the intended purpose and easy to work with. Patterns calling for wool, floss and sometimes chenille can be vastly improved by using natural fur or mohlon. Many such patterns were developed before the use of fur became so wide spread, and mohlon had yet to be invented. Muskrat can be substituted whenever gray fur such as fox, mole, rabbit, etc. is called for. When substituting hooks be certain to use a hook of comparative size and length, otherwise your imitation may not be the intended size. Turkey quills are extremely scarce. I substitute lacquered turkey tail feathers which are a beautiful mottled dark brown color.

Half Hitch

THIS is a simple loop knot used to tie off the head. It is done by throwing a loop around the head and pulling it tight. I like to place two half hitches at the extreme rear of the head. Before cutting the thread, cinch the two knots tight by pulling the thread around the hook eye toward you. When done properly and lacquered with a quality cement there will be no problem with the head coming unraveled. A whip finish is very popular with many tiers and directions are provided with the tool. I recommend the smaller Martarelli or the larger Thompson.

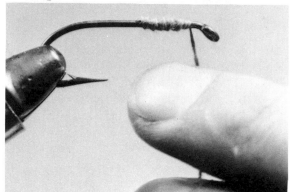 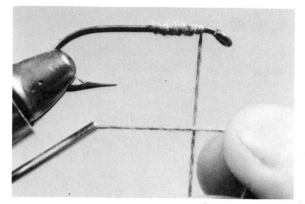

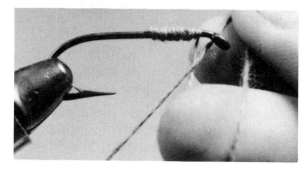

A Word About Fly Patterns

FOR the most part the following patterns are listed as they were originally dressed. When known, the originator's name appears after the name of the fly. Over the years some patterns have evolved differently in certain areas of the country, and many tiers will spot variations in what they are accustomed to seeing. I have tried to include the most widely accepted dressing. I have also taken the liberty of making some minor changes, or improvements if you will, on some patterns. These are most noticeable with floss and wool bodied flies where I highly recommend the use of mohlon or fur.

Many patterns have been tied with a colored thread which compliments the over-all color of the fly. In addition I've used stripped goose on some patterns where a forked tail is called for because goose seems to be the material best suited for this purpose. For many patterns I have listed two or more hooks, thus giving the tier who doesn't have a complete hook selection a couple of suitable alternatives. For tying ease, the parts of the flies have been listed in their tying sequence.

Should anyone notice any outstanding oversights or know of any additional originators please pass the information along to me.

TIMBERLINE EMERGER

Randall Kaufmann

THIS is the best lake emerger I know of. It is so effective that I tie it on a barbless hook for my own use. Several years ago I began looking for an all purpose mayfly emerger which would simulate several hatches in the mountains of the west. My step father, Jack Moore, and I first fished it at Duck Lake. It was nearing August 1st, but at 10,400 feet this deep blue Sierra timberline lake had just shed its coat of ice. A frenzied cloud of mayflies was hatching over a small spring a short cast from the outlet, and in an hour or so we had landed and released several pounds of fat rainbows and headed for camp before dark. The following summers have found me relying more and more on the Timberline Emerger. I rate it as my number one lake fly for rainbow and golden trout.

HOOK:	3906, 3906B 10-14
THREAD:	Gray
TAIL:	Three black moose body hairs
BODY:	Mixture of 30% muskrat and 70% gray seal, other popular colors include tan, brown and olive
WING:	Grizzly hackle tip tied short
HACKLE:	Two turns of brown tied back

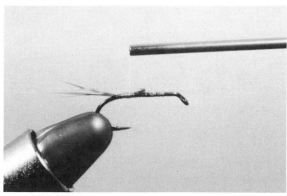

1: Mount three moose fibers for tail

2: Dub on the body forming a good taper

3: Tie in hackle

4: Wrap 2 to 3 turns of hackle and tie off

5: Select two hackle tips for wings and measure proper distance with right hand

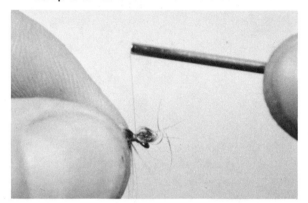

6: Change hands and tie wings in, making sure they are mounted on top of hook, finish off with a neat head and lacquer

SCUD, BROWN

SCUDS are fine additions to any angler's fly box. Besides representing scuds and freshwater shrimp these are often mistaken by the trout for a host of other underwater aquatic life. A wide array of colors and sizes should be carried with both weighted and unweighted varieties included. Swim these across weedy areas or dead drift them down slick runs. Streams like Hot Creek, Silver Creek, Armstrong and eastern limestone waters, etc. are perfect scud waters. Besides the scud colors listed herein, other useful colors include gray brown, gray olive, tan and cream. Experiment a bit.

HOOK:	7957BX 8-16 slightly weighted
TAIL:	Brown hackle fibers tied short
SHELLBACK:	Clear plastic strip
RIB:	Copper wire or monofilament
BODY:	Mixture of 75% brown seal and 25% brown rabbit
ANTENNAE:	Optional, brown hackle fibers

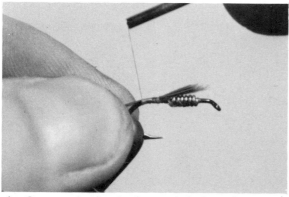

1: Secure the lead wire and tie in a short bunch of brown hackle fibers

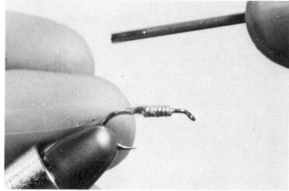

2: Tie in a clear piece of plastic which can be cut from a bag

3: Tie in the copper wire, dub on fur mixture and proceed to wrap body

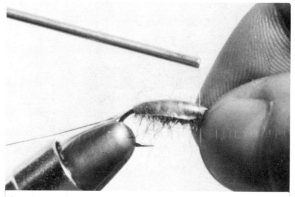

4: Complete body and pull plastic over top of body and secure at head

5: Wind wire over and through the body and secure it at the head

CARROT

HOOK:	3906B 10-16
THREAD:	Orange mono
TAIL:	Black hackle fibers
BODY:	Orange thread
THORAX:	Black chenille or fur
HACKLE:	2 to 3 turns of black

THE carrot has been an old standby for years in the east but it has been slow to catch on in the west. Its halloween colors account for many fat rainbows and brookies from pond and stream alike. I have seen several 3 to 6 pound rainbows and brookies fooled by this fly in Idaho, and I suggest you keep several of these on hand as an ace in the hole. This pattern is a slight variation from the original but quick to tie and very effective. Lookout brookies!

1: Tie in a small, even bunch of black hackle fibers and proceed to build up a tapered thread body

2: Tie in black chenille and build a nice thorax, tie chenille off at the head

3: Tie in black hackle and wrap two to three turns, tie off

4: Grip ALL the fibers of the hackle tip CLOSE to the base, now clip off being sure all fibers are cut in one cut, this will alleviate straggling fibers at the head

TELLICO

REPRESENTING a wide range of trout food, the Tellico has a place in nearly everyone's fly book. It is often used as a last resort and has saved the day for countless anglers. The Tellico fishes well in lake or stream and all species of trout seem to be attracted to it. On a gin clear mountain stream a few summers back I landed cutthroat, rainbow, brown trout and whitefish all in the same pool on a No. 10 Tellico.

HOOK:	3906B 8-14 weighted
THREAD:	Black
TAIL:	3-6 guinea fibers
SHELLBACK:	Ringneck tail fibers
RIB:	Peacock herl (do not rib over shellback, just floss the body)
BODY:	Yellow floss
HACKLE:	Two turns brown hackle

1: Tie in a few wisps of guinea for the tail, select a bunch of ringneck tail fibers and tie in at rear and on top of the hook

2: Tie in a single peacock fiber, now tie in yellow floss

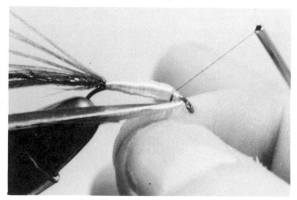

3. Wrap a full floss body and tie off at the head, leaving ample room to complete the head

4: Wrap peacock herl around body as rib and tie it off

5: Pull the ringneck fibers over the top of the body to form the shellback and tie off

6: Tie in a brown hackle and wrap 2 to 3 turns, tie back and finish off a nice head

LONG TAIL MARCH BROWN

BASICALLY an eastern pattern, the Long Tail March Brown has been steadily gaining in popularity west of the rockies, but it still is an eastern favorite for the most part. It's long tail and streamlined body swims nicely in and out of pockets and many anglers like to weight the fly and dead drift it along eddies at dark. The subtle colors are a winning combination which should not be overlooked.

HOOK:	3906B 8-14 weighted
THREAD:	Black
TAIL:	Mallard dyed wood duck 1½ length of body
SHELLBACK:	Mottled brown turkey
RIB:	Yellow tying thread or floss
BODY:	Blended hare's ear
HACKLE:	Brown partridge tied along sides and bottom

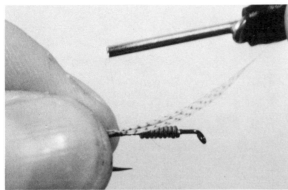

1: Secure lead wire and tie in a long tail of immitation wood duck, tail should curve up and measure 1½ times the length of the body

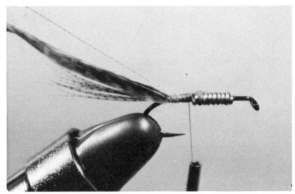

2: Secure shellback at rear of fly and tie in yellow ribbing material

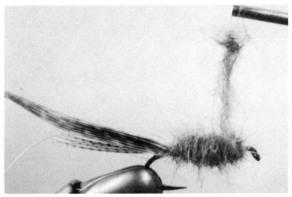

3: Dub on body, keep the body tight so the yellow rib doesn't become lost in the body

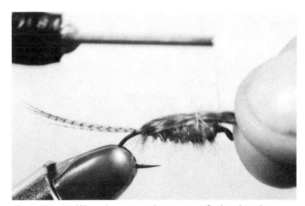

4: Pull shellback over the top of the body and tie down at head

5: Select a good sized bunch of brown partridge and with your right hand set the fibers along both sides and under the body

6: Change hands, gripping the partridge with your left hand, and secure, tie off the head and lacquer

BEAVER

HOOK:	3906B 8-14 weighted
THREAD:	Brown
TAIL:	Gray partridge fibers
RIB:	Gold wire
BODY:	Beaver
BEARD HACKLE:	Gray partridge fibers

THE Beaver nymph is widely used by anglers across the country but it is most popular in the east. The fly is generally weighted and the wire rib adds a little flash and lends a nice segmented look to the body. The Beaver could be termed a simulator pattern and it resembles a wide variety of aquatic life. It is a fine producer on slow limestone streams and it's equally effective in lakes and ponds.

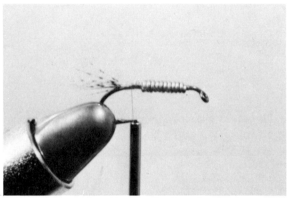

1: After securing the lead wire tie in a small bunch of partridge fibers, be sure all fibers are mounted on top of the hook and are of the same length

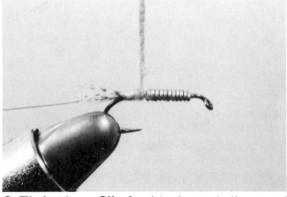

2: Tie in about 3'' of gold wire and clip out of way using a material clip, dub beaver fur onto the thread and proceed to form the body, the dubbing should be tight and a nice taper formed

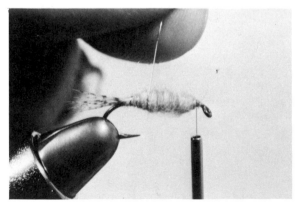

3: Begin to wrap wire around body, evenly spaced, if the wire disappears into the fur body your dubbing was not tight enough, the wire must be plainly visible, tie wire off at the head

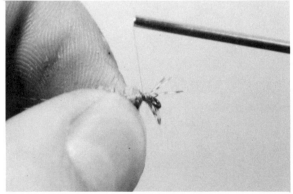

4: Strip off an even bunch of partridge fibers and mount under the body, see Trueblood Shrimp for more detailed instruction, be sure to clip all fibers very close

5: Finish off with a neat head, if there are any fibers protruding from the head you either did a poor job of trimming or you didn't leave enough room for tying in the partridge and completing a nice head, the most common problem with beginning tiers is to crowd the head, leave plenty of room

EMERGENT MOSQUITO

Randall Kaufmann

HOOK:	3906 12-18
THREAD:	Black
TAIL:	Three short fibers of black moose body hair
BODY:	Stripped peacock herl over slight taper of dark fur
THORAX:	Peacock herl
WINGS:	Two grizzly hackle tips tied short over top of thorax

MANY times trout seem to be feeding on adult mosquitos, but a dry fly will only bring refusals. The trout are usually feeding just below the surface on "emerging" mosquitos. This is the reason I came up with the Emergent Mosquito. I would never be without this pattern during the first half of the summer, when nearly every wild creature benefits from the newly hatched mosquitos — especially in the high mountains of the west. This pattern will produce anywhere the pesky varmits are found . . . and you know that's just about everywhere.

Several summers ago I was shivering along a snow rimmed shoreline 11,500 feet high in California's Sierra Nevada Mountains. Ice was crystalizing under my feet and when the evening sun dipped behind a barren peak I was still casting for the elusive golden trout. About dark I dug into my fly box and came up with a fly that resembles the current pattern. With numb fingers I slowly managed a cold knot and three colorful goldens of about a pound each quickly came to my rescue. This fly is certainly worth a try during those mosquito hatches.

1: Tie in three short moose hair fibers for the tail and proceed to dub some dark fur and build up a slight taper as can be seen in the photo

2: Take a peacock fiber and strip off the herl with your thumb and forefinger for about 3/4," now tie in at the rear of the body, lacquer very lightly

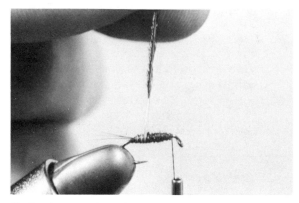 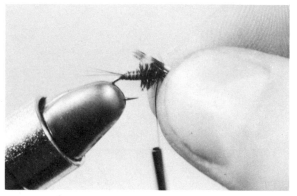

3: Begin wraping the peacock quill forward, the stripped portion of the quill will form the body and the herl will do nicely for the thorax, which should be slightly shorter than the body

4: Pick out two grizzly hackle tips, mount them on top of the hook so they point back over the top of the thorax at the same time making sure they do not extend past the end of the body

---

CATE'S TURKEY

Jerry Cate

THIS small, unobtrusive feather concoction has become a standard killer by "those in the know" throughout Oregon's Cascades. I have fished it throughout the west with unbelievable results and reports from the east are excellent. It suggests a mayfly nymph. The late Jerry Cate consistently took weight limits of fat rainbows in a few hours of fishing. The best method of fishing this nymph is with an incredibly slow "inch" retrive along the bottom of lakes. In running water let the fly swim in eddies and slow water over weed beds.

HOOK:	94845 14-16
THREAD:	Black
TAIL:	A few wisps of mallard fibers dyed wood duck color
RIB:	Gold wire (rib complete fly)
BODY:	Section of dark mottled turkey quill
HEAD:	2 to 3 turns peacock herl
BEARD HACKLE:	Few wisps mallard dyed wood duck

1: Tie in a few wisps of wood duck mallard fibers, then tie in about 3'' of gold wire, keeping the future body area as level as possible, you want to avoid a mound of thread and material at the rear of the hook as this prevents the tier from forming a nicely tapered body

2: Tie in a section of turkey tip first, again keeping the body area level by wraping the tips of the turkey all the way to the area of the head, clip off all excess

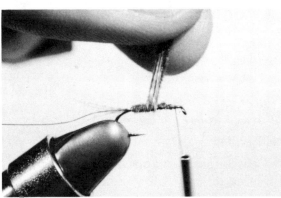

3: Wrap turkey to the head and tie off

4: Tie in peacock herl and take 2 to 3 turns to form the head, tie off

5: Bring gold wire forward and tie off at the head, making sure the wire is tightly and evenly wrapped

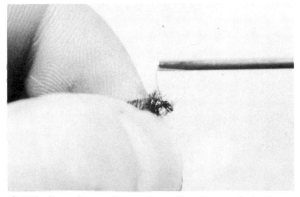

6: Tie in a few wisps of mallard wood duck fibers for beard hackle, being sure fibers do not extend beyond the point of hook, hold the fibers underneath the head and make a loose wrap with the thread, now cinch UP on the fibers and tie off a small, neat head, lacquer

TRUEBLOOD SHRIMP

Ted Trueblood

THIS very simple fly has crept into use on nearly every trout water in the country, being especially popular for lake fishing when casting for "cruisers" over weed beds and drop-offs. It is also very effective when crept across the bottom of lakes or drifted in spring creeks. The buggy translucence of seal and otter has accounted for many a trout at the end of a dancing rod. The other color variations are also quite effective and should not be overlooked.

HOOK:	7957BX, 3906, 3906B 8-16 weighted
THREAD:	Brown unweighted, green weighted
TAIL:	Brown partridge fibers
BODY:	50/50 mixture of otter and natural cream seal
BEARD HACKLE:	Brown partridge fibers
NOTE:	Outstanding variations are tied with black rabbit mixed with black seal, or muskrat mixed with gray seal

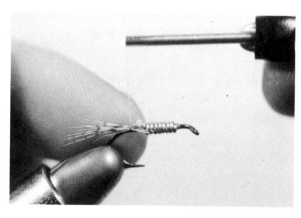

1: Apply and secure the lead wire, select a bunch of partridge fibers, these can easily be pulled off one side of the feather, leaving the other side for the beard hackle, tie directly on top of the hook as can be seen in the photo, all the fibers should be about the same length

2: Dub the body material on the thread and begin wrapping the body, making sure there is a slight taper, the over-all body can be a little bit on the heavy side.

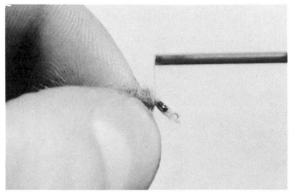

3: Pull off a bunch of partridge fibers as in the tail, hold the fibers in your right hand and place under the body, check for the proper length, fibers should not extend past the point of the hook

4: Now grip the hackle with your left hand and secure, tie off the head

BLACK HELGRAMITE

Doug Prince

THIS is one of the best helgramite patterns. It comes from the inventive bench of Doug Prince and has proven itself time and again for me. Trout from the Deschutes, Owens, Madison, Yellowstone, Williamson, Klamath, Kings and countless other streams seem to go out of their way to gobble this big nymph. The nymph itself is very time consuming to tie so it is not popular with commercial tiers and seldom available "over the counter." Tie up an assortment of these and show them to Mrs. Trout.

HOOK:	3665A, 79580, 9672 6-10 weighted
THREAD:	Black
TAIL:	Black stripped goose tied short and slightly down in a "V"
RIB:	Optional
BODY:	Black floss, mohlon or other yarn or swiss straw
WINGCASE:	Gray or black goose wing quill section
THORAX:	Black rabbit palmered with 3 to 4 turns black saddle hackle with strip of red wool along the underbody
LEGS:	Black stripped goose fibers tied along the sides of the body with tips flaring out and extending about half the length of the body

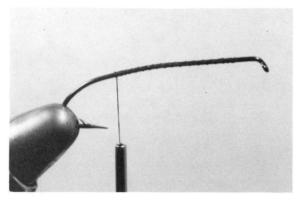

1: After mounting the hook in the vise give it a slight bend as seen in above photo, secure lead wire

2: Tie in a "V" tail of stripped goose, keep the tail short and pointed slightly downward, tie in the black ostrich, next secure black floss and begin wrapping a tight, tapered body

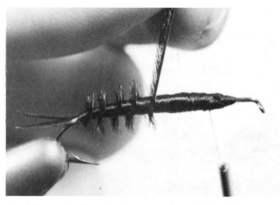

3: After the b ody is completed, begin wrapping ostrich around the body, tie off in the thorax section and clip ostrich close to body

4: Tie in a section of goose quill feather and mount it directly on top of the body

5: Now secure black saddle hackle and mount a piece of red wool along the underside of thorax

6: Dub on black rabbit and form the thorax

7: Wrap 3 to 4 turns of hackle through the thorax and tie off, pull red wool along underside of body and secure at the head, you are now ready to bring over the wing-case and tie it off at the head

8: Select two stripped goose fibers and mount along sides of thorax so that the tips flare away from the body as in the photo

TIMBERLINE

Randall Kaufmann

T HE Timberline came about a few years ago for the purpose of filling a gap in my assortment of high lake flies. In many timberline lakes the mayfly nymph is all that carries the fish through the long winters and they are accustomed to feeding freely on these small wrigglers. It was after I observed two beautifully colored rainbow-golden cross trout crusing a shallow inlet area picking up mayfly nymphs along the bottom that I began to experiment with a suitably suggestive pattern. When slightly weighted and inched across the bottom of drop-offs, or drifted down an inlet the timberline is deadly. While it is not an exact immitation, fish seem to mistake it for several brownish colored mayfly nymphs and that is its intended purpose. It produces anywhere mayflies are found.

HOOK:	3906B, 10-18 weighted
THREAD:	Brown
TAIL:	3 moose body hair fibers tied short
RIB:	Copper wire
BODY:	Fur from a hare's ear clipped directly from the ears and not matted, body colors can be varied
WINGCASE:	Dark side of a ringneck pheasant tail
THORAX:	Same as body
LEGS:	Few ringneck tail fibers along each side of body

45

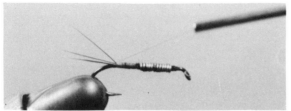

1: Secure wire and tie in three black moose fibers keeping them short and slightly spread out, often a tail can be easily spread out by taking a wrap of thread or fur behind the tail, this will often give it a slight lift upwards

2: Tie in copper wire, dub hare's ear on thread and form the body, keeping it tight so the wire won't become lost in the fur

3: Wind the wire rib through the body and tie off

4: Tie in section of pheasant tail, dub more fur and wrap on the thorax

5: Bring the wingcase over the thorax, secure and tie off

6: Select 6 fibers from a ringneck tail and place three along each side of the body

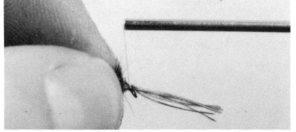

7: When the legs are in place grip with your left hand and secure, clip off excess, complete head and lacquer, pick out thorax fur if desired

MATT'S FUR

Matt Lavell

THIS natural appearing nymph soon becomes a favorite with anyone lucky enough to come by the pattern. The shape and translucent body adds up to one of my favorites. It seems to be especially suited to rainbows, and many of the beautiful redsides have fallen prey to the Matt's Fur. I prefer to fish it in heavier riffles.

HOOK:	9575, 9672, 9671 6-12 weighted
THREAD:	Brown
TAIL:	Mallard dyed wood duck
RIB:	Oval gold tinsel
BODY:	50-50 mixture of otter and cream seal
WINGCASE:	Same as tail
THORAX:	Same as body
HACKLE:	Left over tips of wingcase are pulled back along the sides and bottom of the fly. These legs should not extend beyond the point of the hook.

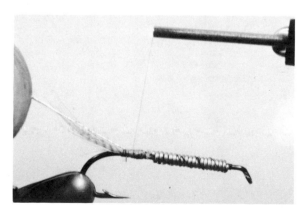

1: Secure lead wire, tie in tail and a piece of oval tinsel

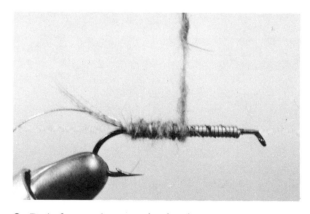

2: Dub fur and wrap the body

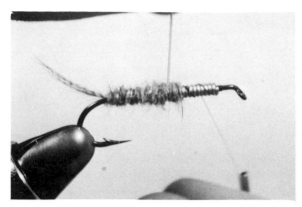

3: Wind tinsel evenly through the body and tie off at the thorax

4: Tie in the wingcase feather, allowing for the legs, basic rule is to make sure the wingcase feather extends to the rear of the tail, assuming your tail is of the proper length, dub more fur and form a nice buggy tapered thorax

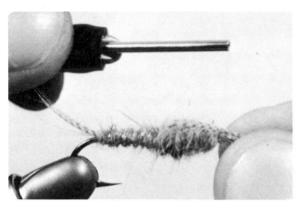

5: Bring wingcase feather over the top of the thorax and secure it at the head, do not clip off the ends

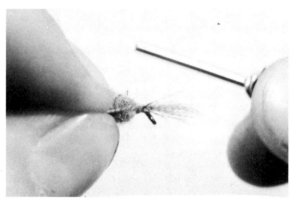

6: Split the leftover wingcase tips in half and tie them back along the sides of the body, finish off head, lacquer, and pick out fur under thorax

TROUT SHRIMP

Randall Kaufmann

I N A FEW waters trout grow at a phenomenal rate, sometimes putting on two or more pounds in a year. Such waters usually have an astounding population of fresh water shrimp and the trout are constantly gorging themselves. Shrimp are generally brownish tan to grayish green in color and range in size from 8 to 18. A shrimp will turn pink in color after spawning or when dead. For protection a shrimp will curl up like a sow bug but they are more often than not stretched out to full length swimming or crawling along. Shrimp are most commonly found in spring creeks, meadow lakes and some high mountain lakes. The Trout Shrimp is a fine producer wherever shrimp are found.

HOOK:	7957BX 14-16 slightly weighted
THREAD:	Gray
TAIL:	Mallard flank
SHELLBACK:	Mallard flank
RIB:	Silver wire
BODY:	50-50 mixture of muskrat and gray seal
FEELERS:	Mallard flank

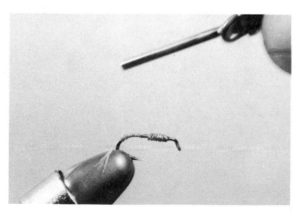

1: Secure wire on front portion of hook and tie in a few tail fibers around the bend of the hook as in the photo

2: Tie in the shellback right at the tail, next tie in the silver wire

3: Dub body material and form the body, tie
   off at the head

 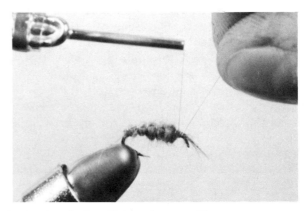

4,5: Pull shellback over the top of the body, tie it off but do not clip
off the tips which should be about the same length as the tail, it will take
a little practice to judge the length of the shellback so that the tips come
out to the proper length, wrap the wire over the body keeping the shellback on top of the body, tie off

6: Wrap thread in front of antennae so fibers
   point forward, and slightly up, finish head

OLIVE SEDGE

THIS is a very useful pattern when caddis flies are hatching, for this fly imitates the emergers just before they reach the surface. Many times a dry caddis imitation will bring only refusals, but an emerging pattern will fool many fish. In some areas caddis flies are referred to as sedges but they are the same insect. These will be noticed in several sizes and colors so the wise fisherman should have a wide selection of sedge-like emergers. Keep the wingcase, legs and thorax the same, only changing the color of the body. Browns, yellows and various shades of green are some of the more effective variations. Caddis hatches are quite prolific and often appear early in the summer and continue right through autumn.

HOOK: 3906, 3906B 10-16
THREAD: Brown
BODY: Olive rabbit (mix a little green seal for a translucent buggy effect)
WINGCASE: Gray duck quill sections tied along both sides of the body and extending from
               1/2 to 3/4 length of body
BEARD HACKLE: Brown partridge tied in before thorax
THORAX: Hare's ear

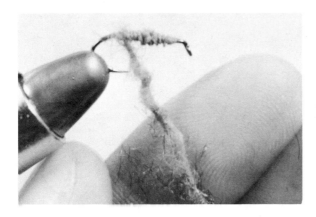

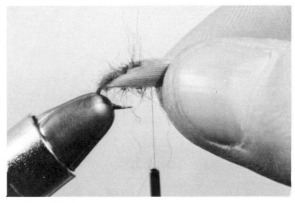

1: Begin to dub on the body, if desired one can dub some seal fur over the rabbit for an added effect, the seal will adhere easily to the rabbit

2: Clip a section of duck wing quill from a left and right side (two different feathers) and hold in place with your right hand, this will enable you to judge the distance correctly, now grab the material with your left hand and secure it in place

3: Tie in partridge in the same manner judging the distance with your left hand

4: Grab the partridge and secure it as shown, the hackle should extend to the hook point

5: Dub more fur on the thread and wrap the thorax as shown, the thorax is comparatively small and is actually more like a "head," tie off and lacquer

LINGREN'S OLIVE

Ira Lingren

IRA LINGREN lived in the Sierra foothills and developed several sparsely tied nymphs which are of value to fishermen everywhere. Over the past twenty odd years his patterns have been tested on all kinds of trout from the waters of the Arctic to the small desert streams of the southwest. Lingren's olive is a subtle pattern which often does the trick for me — especially on hard fished waters. Trout often mistake it for a small mayfly nymph and it should be fished accordingly — very slow.

HOOK:	3906B 10-18
THREAD:	Black
TAIL:	Black hackle fibers
RIB:	Gold wire
THORAX:	Peacock herl
HACKLE:	2 to 3 turns black hackle clipped top and bottom

1: Tie in tail and piece of gold wire, it desired you can build up the body with a slight amount of fur but this pattern was originally tied sparse

2: Tie in several fibers of olive marabou tip first at the tail, by doing this a slight taper is insured as the marabou fibers are smaller at the tips than at the base

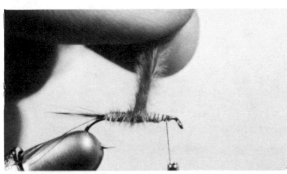

3: Wrap the marabou for the body and tie it off

4: Tie in peacock and wrap the thorax, tie off

5: Wind the wire through the body and thorax making sure it's evenly and tightly wrapped

6: Tie in the black hackle and make 2 to 3 turns, tie off, finish off small, neat head and clip the hackle top and bottom, leaving a few wisps along each side

BITCH CREEK

AT first glance the Bitch Creek will draw a smile and perhaps even a snear from a fly fisherman's poker face — thinking the fly is some kind of a joke. One look at the ungainly feelers, tail and oversized body should draw a smile out of a bullhead. Since my introduction to the Bitch Creek over ten years ago on the Madison, I have come to respect those rubber legs and plump body. This fly has a habit of dredging up the big fish from big water. The rubber legs pulsate madly and this must drive the fish crazy. Many fishermen like to weight this fly with extra heavy lead and bounce it along the bottom.

HOOK:	9575, 9672, 79580 2-8 weighted
THREAD:	Black
TAIL:	2 white rubber legs
BODY:	Black chenille with strip of orange chenille pulled underneath the body and secured by crisscrossing the thread back over the body
THORAX:	Black chenille palmered with 3 to 4 turns of brown saddle hackle
FEELERS:	Same as tail

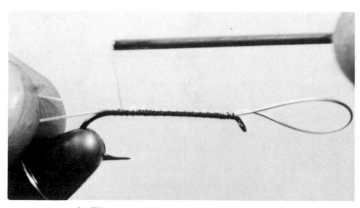

1: Tie on rubber legs and feelers

2: Tie in 2″ piece of orange chenille along the underside of the hook at the tail

3: Tie in black chenille and wrap all the way to the head, tie off and wrap thread back to the rear of the thorax area, bring orange chenille along the underside of the body and tie it down

4: Wrap the thread to the rear in about five turns and bring it forward again, this creates an "X" pattern over the body and secures the orange chenille

5: Tie in brown saddle hackle at rear of thorax, now tie in black chenille and build up a fat thorax and tie off at head

6: Wrap 3 to 4 turns of hackle, palmer style, through the thorax and tie off, complete the head and lacquer

GREEN MOUNTAIN DAMSEL

Ranfall Kaufmann

DAMSEL nymphs are a relished bonus to a trout's diet and trout feed freely on these whenever one happens by. Lakes which have an abundance of damsel flies usually have a large population of hefty trout. Damsels flies are scattered from the boggy ponds of the Maine woods to the lowland lakes of the damp Pacific coast. Damsel nymphs are best fished in weedy areas, and a well placed cast among some cattails will often lure out a lunker brookie or rainbow. Many waters in British Columbia harbor an incredible population of damsels, and a fisherman drifting in that direction should have a large stock in his vest. Damsel nymphs also account for many land locked Atlantic salmon in the northeast.

Note: Keep the bodies as slim as possible.

HOOK: 9575, 9672 8-14
THREAD: Olive
TAIL: Olive stripped goose tied short in a "V"
SHELLBACK: Olive marabou
RIB: Gold wire
BODY: Dark green seal
WING: Olive marabou tied to 1/3 the length of the body

Note: Tie body very slim with slight taper. A brown olive color
      is another good choice.

1: Tie in the stripped goose tail in a "V",
   next select several olive marabou fibers
   and tie them in at rear of hook, the marabou will form the shellback

2: Tie in gold wire and build up a slight taper
   of fur as an underbody

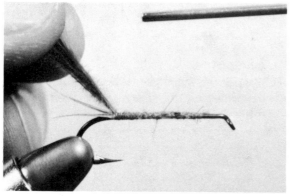

3: Dub on olive seal for the body

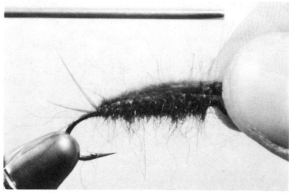

4: Pull the marabou over the top of the body
   to form the shellback, secure it at the head

5: Wind the wire through the body keeping the shellback positioned on top of the body — not to either side, be certain the rib is even and tightly wound

6: Tie in a short fluff of marabou for the wing and clip to 1/3 the length of the body, tie off the head and pick out the seal body in the area of the thorax, this will lend a buggy appearance to the fly, lacquer the head

BLACK MARTINEZ

Don Martinez

HOOK:	3906B 8-14
THREAD:	Black
TAIL:	Few guinea fibers
RIB:	Oval gold tinsel
BODY:	Black seal
WINGCASE:	Green raffia
THORAX:	Black chenille
HACKLE:	Mallard flank

THE Black Martinez is very attractive to fishermen along with being a first class trout getter. It originated in the Yellowstone area and has spread to just about every corner of the country and into Canada. This fly accounts for many rainbows, brookies, and browns throughout the season and should be carried in a wide array of sizes, especially by those anglers visiting the Rockies.

1: Tie in guinea fibers for the tail, now tie in 2" or so of tinsel

2: Dub on black seal, dub on loosely and a little at a time

3: Wrap tinsel through body tight and evenly

4: Tie in green wingcase material on top of hook, now secure the black chenille

5: Build up a nice fat thorax with the chenille and tie it off

6: Pull wingcase over thorax and tie it off

7: Select a good bunch of mallard and place it around thorax, be sure the fibers form a complete circle around the thorax

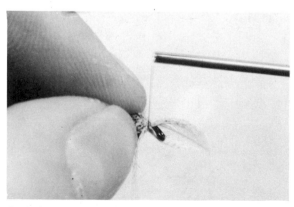

8: Grip the fibers with your left hand and secure with tying thread, complete head and lacquer

BROWN FORKED TAIL

Doug Prince

T HE Prince nymph was developed 35 years ago by California tier Doug Prince. The last ten years have seen this pattern take hold just about everywhere. In larger sizes it is deadly on big rainbows and ranks as a national favorite. It's sparse dressing allows it to sink down into deep, dark pockets and it should be stocked in assorted sizes.

HOOK:	9671, 9672 4-12 weighted
THREAD:	Black
TAIL:	Brown stripped goose tied in a "V" and not too long
RIB:	Flat gold tinsel
BODY:	Peacock herl
HACKLE:	2 to 4 turns dark brown
WING:	White stripped goose tied in a "V" over the top of the body so the tips flare up

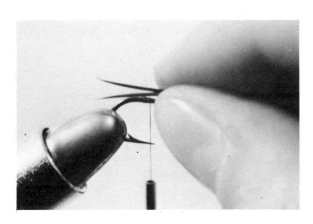 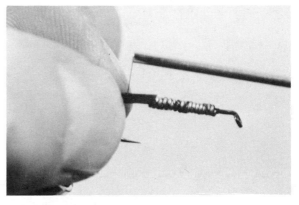

1:,2: Secure wire, select two brown stripped goose fibers and tie them in for the tail, measure the desired distance by holding the fibers in place with your right hand, change hands and tie them in

3: Tie in a piece of flat gold tinsel and clip it out of way in material clip, now tie in 4 thick peacock herls and wrap a juicy, tapered body

4: Wrap the tinsel through the body to form the rib, making sure the tinsel is evenly wrapped and tight

5: Tie in the hackle and wrap 2 to 4 turns, tie the hackle back in wet fly fashion

6: Select two fibers of stripped goose and lay them over the top of the fly as shown in the photo, grip the two fibers with your left hand and tie in, finish off the head, take care to notice the proper proportions of the fly and the uncrowded head, lacquer head

BIRD'S STONE FLY, BROWN

FEW flies can compete with the Birds Stone Fly in the taking of big trout. This nymph is especially effective during the famous salmon fly hatch. The hatch occurs on several western trout waters, usually beginning in June on Pacific coast streams, and a couple of weeks later in the Rockies. Fish up to 25 inches are fairly common at this time. The knowledgeable angler will work upstream of the main hatch, as the fish will be feeding on the nymphs as they make their way to the bank to emerge into adults. This fly is most effective when fished along the bottom, and no western angler can afford to be without it.

HOOK:	9575, 9672, 79580 4-10 weighted
THREAD:	Orange
TAIL:	Brown stripped goose tied in a "V"
RIB:	Orange thread
BODY:	Beaver or mohlon tied with "twist" method
WINGCASE:	Turkey quill
THORAX:	Peacock herl palmered with 3 to 4 turns of brown saddle hackle

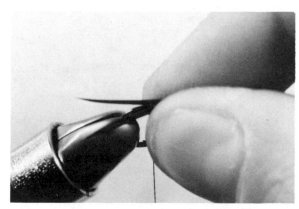

1: Secure wire and tie in the tail in a "V", mount the goose fibers along each side of the hook so the tips flare away from each other as shown in the photo, hold the fibers in place with your right hand to judge the proper distance, switch hands and tie in place as in photo No. 2.

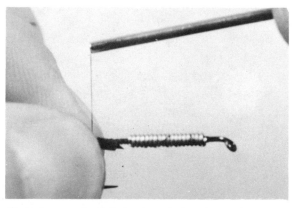

2: It is very helpful when tying in various materials to grip the feather right at the tie down point, next, bring the thread UP between your two fingers and cinch down

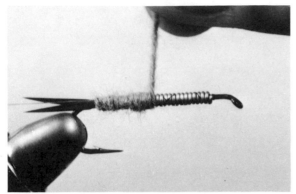

3: Tie in thread for the rib and clip it out of the way

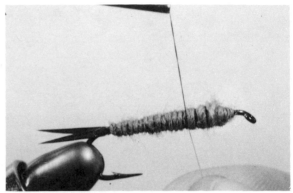

4: Bring the thread rib through the body following the grooves of the mohlon, tie off

5: Tie in turkey wing case on top of the hook, hook, then the brown saddle hackle (strip fibers off the lower ¼") and finally tie in about 4 strands of peacock herl

6: Wrap peacock for the thorax, tie off and then wrap 3 to 4 turns of hackle over the thorax

7: Tie off the hackle

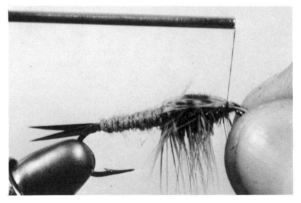

8: Bring turkey over the thorax and hackle to form the wingcase, groom the hackle to make sure there are no "wild" fibers sticking out of the wingcase or head, finish off with a neat head

SUPER GRAY

Howard Eskin

THE Super Gray is definitely a simulator pattern and it comes from the bench of Howard Eskin of New York. Its colors are extremely natural and coupled with its exquisite action the fly makes for a winning combination. While the pattern is not very wide spread, it is worth a try in your favorite water. Fish it with lots of action and swim it across the riffles.

HOOK: 7957BX 2-12
THREAD: Black
TAIL: Mallard dyed wood duck
SHELLBACK: 2 to 6 strands of peacock
RIB: Gold wire
BODY: Gray mohlon palmered with grizzly hackle clipped off on top
WING: Red (fox) squirrel tail extending about to the bend of the hook

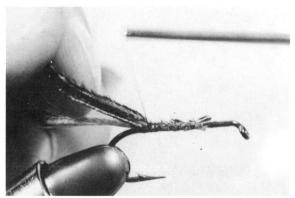

1: Secure the tail, tie in a few strands of peacock herl and clip out of the way using material clip

2: Tie in section of gold wire, clip out of the way and tie in a long grizzly saddle hackle, next, tie in the gray mohlon, proceed to wrap the body with the gray mohlon and tie it off at head

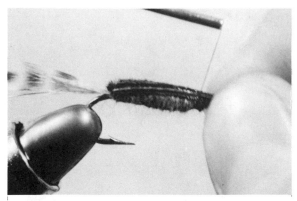

3: Bring the peacock herl over the top of the body to form the shellback and tie it off at head

4: Wind the gold wire through the body making sure it is evenly spaced and tightly wound, now wrap the hackle up to head and tie it off

5. Trim the hackle on top of the body

6,7: Place squirrel tail wing over the top of the body with your left hand, judge the proper distance, change hands and tie off, finish off with a neat head and lacquer

MONTANA STONE

THE Montana Stone is without a doubt one of the most popular nymphs in use today. It is a common sight in fly boxes from east to west. Big fish accept this for various stoneflies and especially for the black willow stonefly which is indigenous to nearly all larger running trout waters. The stronghold of this fly, naturally enough, is Montana, where the fly regularly accounts for monster trout. Its fame has spread into Canada, and the angler would do well to have an assortment tucked away in his fly book.

HOOK:	9575, 9672, 79580 6-10 weighted
THREAD:	Black
TAIL:	Black hackle fibers
BODY:	Black chenille
WINGCASE:	2 strands black chenille
THORAX:	Yellow chenille palmered with three turns black saddle hackle

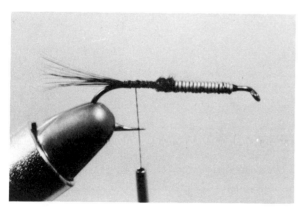

1: Secure the lead wire and tie in a bunch of black hackle fibers for the tail, be sure the hackle fibers are all the same length

2: Tie in a 3″ piece of black chenille and wrap it slightly past the half way point on the hook, forming the body

3: Tie in two strips of black chenille on top of the hook, select the proper size of black saddle hackle and strip off the fibers for about ¼" as shown in the photo, by doing this the first wrap of hackle will flare out at right angles from the thorax instead of looking sloppy and scattered

4,5: Tie in a 3" section of yellow chenille and build up the thorax by continuing the body taper, tie it off at the head but be sure to leave enough room for a neat tapered head

6: Wrap 3 to 4 turns of black hackle through the thorax, tie it off at the head and clip off ALL stray hackle fibers as closely as possible

7: Bring the two chenille strips over the top of the thorax and black hackle, tie off and groom the hackle so there are no stray fibers protruding up through the wingcase or out from the head, finish off with a neat head and lacquer

R.K. MAYFLY

Randall Kaufmann

THE R. K. Mayfly is an all purpose nymph that simulates several brownish colored nymphs found throughout North America. I fish it with consistent results in lowland streams and mountain lakes by letting it swim slowly with the current or with short retrieves in lakes. The mono ribbing should be evenly spaced, far enough apart to allow the ostrich to protrude. The mono rib also lends a fine segmented look to the body while the ostrich looks like breathing gills. This, coupled with the buggy thorax, is a winning combination. All that is needed is running water and a trout or two.

HOOK:	3906B 10-16 weighted
THREAD:	Black or brown
TAIL:	Three dark moose body hairs
RIB:	4-10 lb. monofilament (preferably shaded brown, not clear)
BODY:	Brown ostrich
WINGCASE:	Dark speckled hen or turkey
THORAX:	Brown mink picked out to simulate legs

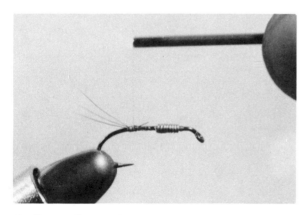

1: Secure lead wire and mount the three fibered tail

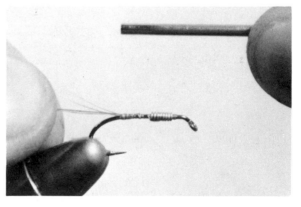

2: Tie in the monofilament along the side of the hook and secure it tightly at the rear of the fly

3: Tie in the brown ostrich, dub some fur and build up an even taper keeping it slim, this will allow the monofilament to wind evenly and will lend a natural appearance to the body

4: Wrap the ostrich forward to the thorax area and tie off

5: Wrap on the monofilament, allowing lots of ostrich to show through

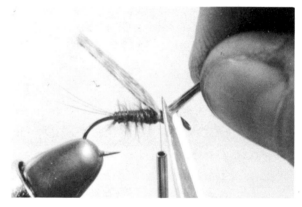

6: Tie in the wingcase and clip off any excess as closely as possible

7: Dub mink and build up the thorax

8: Bring the wingcase over the thorax and secure it at head, complete the head, tie it off and lacquer

HARE'S EAR, GOLD RIBBED

HOOK:	3906B 8-16 weighted
THREAD:	Brown
TAIL:	Hare's ear, taken from ears or mask and tied short
RIB:	Oval gold tinsel
BODY:	Blended hare's ear
WINGCASE:	Mottled brown turkey
THORAX:	Blended hare's ear picked out to suggest legs

THE Hare's Ear is a buggy simulator pattern which has received an abundance of publicity over the past few years. The pattern has become an all time favorite and is an outstanding producer just about everywhere. When crept across the bottom, the trout is most likely to take it for a mayfly nymph, but it is a killer no matter how it is fished. Every serious fly fisherman from the small streams of the Catskills to the dense rain forests of the Pacific Northwest carries a wide selection of Hare's Ears.

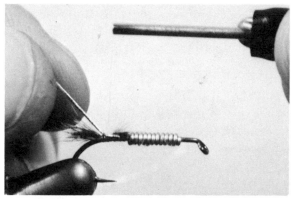

1: Secure lead wire and tie in a short fluff of hair and fur from a hare's mask, the tail should be short with all the fibers the same length, next tie in a 3" piece of gold oval tinsel

2: Dub on hare's ear fur, hare's ear is best worked with when it has been blended, when clipping off the fur to be blended avoid using the real light fur, clip the ears especially close, form the body and wrap the tinsel over the body and tie it off at the thorax

3: Tie in a segment of turkey quill as shown in the photo, making sure it's secure back over the body, dub more fur and build up a nice thorax

4: After the thorax is completed pull the turkey quill over the top to form the wing-case

5: Secure the wingcase at the head and clip off any excess, finish off the head and pick out some of the fur to depict the legs

BLACK CADDIS EMERGER

T HE latter half of the summer finds thousands of blackish brown caddis flies fluttering over my favorite backcountry waters. I had never been very successful with dry flies during this hatch, so I set about to develop a suitable "emerger" for the next season. Over the long winter months I came up with the current version.

My first chance to fish it came in Wyoming, in a snow choked lake basin, under the shadow of the continental divide. Much to my delight the fat cutthroats were easy victims, and many rainbows, brooks and goldens have since felt its sharp point. The Black Caddis Emerger is an excellent pattern wherever this hatch occurs.

HOOK: 3906B 10-16

THREAD: Black

TAIL: 3 moose body hair fibers (black) tied short (tail optional but adds stability)

BODY: "Twisted" black mohlon or rabbit

THORAX: Black rabbit palmered with black hackle clipped short on top and to the gap of hook on bottom

WINGCASE: Lacquered black duck wing segment clipped to form a sharp "V" on the top and along sides

1: Tie in three fibers for the tail and build a tapered fur underbody, next tie in a length of black mohlon at the rear and using the "twist" method wrap the body onto the thorax

2: Tie in a black hackle

3: Dub on black fur and build up the thorax

4: Wind 3 to 4 turns of black hackle through the thorax and tie it off

 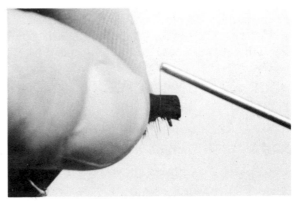

5: Clip off the hackle on the top and to the gap of the hook on the bottom

6: Select a section of brownish black duck quill segment and mount on top of hook for wing, complete the head

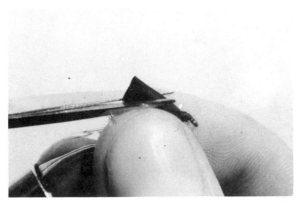 

7: Clip wing to a "V" about 1/3 the length of the body

8: Clip the sides of the wing at a slant as shown in the above photo, lacquer the head

RANDALL'S CADDIS

Randall Kaufmann

THIS caddis nymph is quite simple in construction and closely resembles the actual nymph. Caddis nymphs are very wide spread and form a major part of a trout's diet. Since there are about 1,000 species found in North America one can only wonder at the size and coloration available to the fish. The browns, yellows, greens and black are perhaps the most useful.

The nymphs will have a definite segmentation to the body, so I use the "twist" method of construction. For a more curved effect on the body, start the body on the bend of the hook. Many of these caddis in the larger sizes are quite fat so a tapered underbody is desirable or one can double the mohlon for about the same effect. Nymphs can be fished by creeping them across the bottom or by a free drift method. Most caddis have a protective casing and fish will eat them case and all, but a caddis without its case is a definite victim.

HOOK: 3906B, 7957BX 6-14 weighted
THREAD: Black
RIB: Copper wire (rib entire body and thorax)
BODY: Mohlon tied with the "twist" method, popular colors are browns, greens,
             yellows, gray and black, for a more curved effect, start the body back on the
             hook bend
THORAX: Peacock and black ostrich wound together
BEARD HACKLE: Few wisps of black hackle fibers

1: Secure lead wire, tie in fine copper wire for rib and clip out of the way, next mount mohlon along the underside of the hook beginning at the end of the lead wire, this will even out the body and give it a better taper

2: Twist the mohlon and thread together and wrap the body, tie off at the head area

3: Tie in a strand of peacock and ostrich

4: Wrap the peacock and ostrich forming the thorax, thorax should be ¼ the length of the body or less, tie off

5: Bring copper wire through the body and thorax as rib, the wire will follow the segments of the body creating a nice subtle effect

6: Mount a few black hackle fibers along the underside of the body so they extend to the hook point but not beyond

---

CAREY SPECIAL

Tom Carey

HOOK:	9575, 9671, 9672 6-14
THREAD:	Black
TAIL:	Ringneck rump or tail fibers
RIB:	Any color fine wire
BODY:	Can be most anything, peacock, ringneck tail fibers, wool, floss, etc.
HACKLE:	Same as tail, tied full and long

FLY fishermen in the northwest and Canada are quite familiar with the Carey Special, as it is probably the most popular nymph and is readily available in most shops. Many people fish it as a streamer or wet fly, but it was originated as an imitation of the damsel fly nymph. The fly is useful in simulating a lot of trout food and some of my friends on the east coast would do well to experiment with a few of these. The hackle has a lot of breathing action, and it should be fished in a darting or swimming manner. It is also effective when crept across the bottom.

1: Build up a tapered fur underbody and mount the tail

2: Tie in a section of pheasant tail

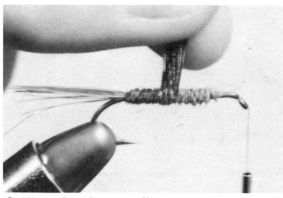

3: Wrap the pheasant fibers around the hook shank as far as possible and tie off, on smaller flies this should be enough to cover the body, on larger flies it may be necessary to tie in another clump of pheasant to complete the body

4: Tie in another clump of pheasant fibers and wrap toward the eye of hook, tie off

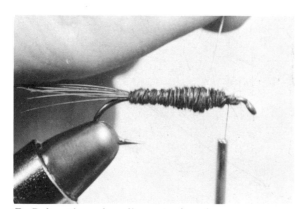

5: Bring the wire rib up to head area

6: Select an even clump of pheasant tail fiber and mount over the top of the body, take another clump and mount it along the sides until the material encircles the entire body, this is referred to as the hackle, tie off and lacquer the head

ZUG BUG

T HE Zug Bug is another old standby with quite a reputation. Its fame has crept into Canadian waters and it is a number one favorite in the states. No selection of nymphs would be complete without a few Zug Bugs. I have taken just about every kind of trout, and a few trash fish to boot, on this predominately peacock dressed pattern. If you haven't already found this one give it a try.

HOOK:	3906B 8-14
THREAD:	Black
TAIL:	3-6 peacock sword fibers
RIB:	Flat or oval silver tinsel
BODY:	Peacock herl
WING:	Mallard dyed wood duck clipped to 1/3 body length
BEARD HACKLE:	Brown hackle fibers

1: Tie in the tail, the tail should not be too long

2: Tie in the tinsel, dub on a little fur and build up a slight underbody so the fly will have a good taper

3: Tie in a few strands of peacock herl and proceed to wrap body, tie it off at the head

4: Wrap tinsel through the body keeping it evenly spaced and tight

5: Select a nice clump of brown hackle fibers and hold them in place with the right hand

6: Change hands and secure them in place under the hook

7: Tie in a clump of mallard dyed wood duck and mount it on top of hook, clip off, trimming it to 1/3 the length of the body

KAUFMANN'S BROWN STONE

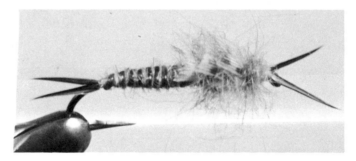

THE giant stoneflies mean two things: a big mouthful for trout and big trout for fishermen. The most common colored stoneflies in the west are the golden, brown and black. The brown is often referred to as a salmonfly, while the black is mislabeled a helgramite. All three are readily taken by trout, and the fisherman should be well armed with these. While they are effective the entire season they are most deadly just prior to and during the early stages of the hatch. The goldens and browns hatch out in the spring and are the first big attraction to many fishermen and to many fish. The flat monofilament rib lends a perfect segmented effect while the seal gives life to the fly.

HOOK:	9575 2-10 weighted (flatten lead wire with pliers)
THREAD:	Brown
TAIL:	Brown stripped goose tied very short
RIB:	Dyed dark brown flat monofilament
BODY:	Mix dark brown seal and dark brown tabbit with a bit of claret, purple, black and orange seal—clip off excess after rib is in place
WINGCASE:	Mottled turkey tied in three separate sections along the top of the thorax and clipped to a "V" on top
THORAX:	Same as body
ANTENNAE:	Brown stripped goose

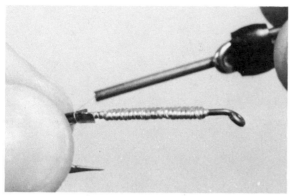

1: Secure the lead wire on the forward section of the hook and flatten with pliers, now mount the tail

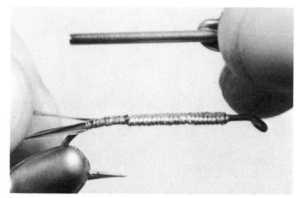

2: Tie in the monofilament along the side of the hook and wrap it all the way to the tail making sure it won't slip

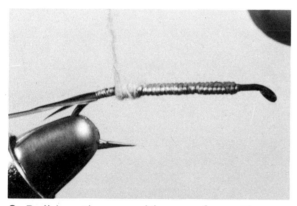

3: Build up the rear with some fur so there is a taper between the lead wire and the tail, this will give the monofilament a smooth base to cover

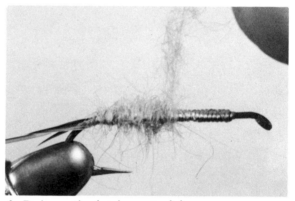

4: Dub on the body material

5: Bring the rib up to the thorax area

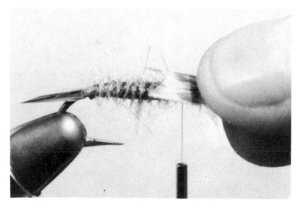

6: Select a section of turkey (it is best to lacquer it before tying) and clip the end in a "V" as is shown in the photo, judge the proper distance with your right hand

7: Secure the case in place, making sure you have wrapped the thread back onto the body, and that the end of the case is approximately at the halfway point of the hook

8: Dub on some more fur and build a section of thorax, now prepare another case section and tie it in as before

9: Dub on another section of thorax and prepare the final wingcase

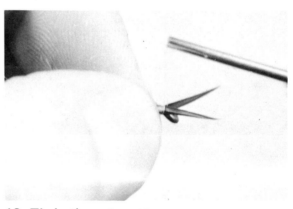

10: Tie in the antennae

11: Dub on more body material and form the head, tie off and lacquer

12: Clip off the seal close to the body and groom the thorax (the body may be clipped after the rib is in place if desired)

RANDALL'S
GREEN DRAGON

Randall Kaufmann

DRAGON flies are quite numerous and provide a giant mouthful for just about any size trout. Many lunker fish have fallen to such imitations in lakes and streams alike. The Green Dragon is a recent development of mine, tied to closely duplicate the actual insect. This colored dragon fly nymph *(Anax junius)* is very popular with the fish and is also quite widespread. The tying of this pattern is rather involved, but the rewards will be well worth your time. The fly is very productive along the Pacific coast and is being experimented with for steelhead trout. It shouldn't be overlooked in eastern and Canadian waters.

THREAD:	Olive
TAIL:	Olive stripped goose tied in "V" extremely short
RIB:	Clear flat monofilament
BODY:	Mixture of 40% olive rabbit and 60% insect green seal (clip short after rib)
LEGS:	Olive stripped goose tied at the front of the body extending back along sides of the body to the halfway point with tips curving in toward the body
THORAX:	Same as the body
WINGCASE:	Olive duck quill segment tied down at the rear of the thorax and the front with approximately ¼" extending out over the body and clipped to a "V"
LEGS:	Olive stripped goose tied in front of the thorax and extending back along the sides to end of the wingcase, tips of the goose should curve in toward the body
HEAD:	Same as the body

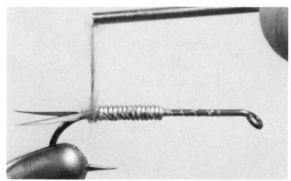

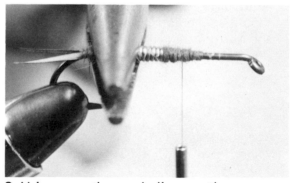

1: Secure lead wire on the extreme rear half of the hook, this should be flattened to imitate the body shape of the natural, tie in the tail along the sides of the hook keeping it very short, next dub a little olive fur and build a slight taper at the rear and front of the wire, see photo No. 2, this is advisable to be certain that the flat mono will cover evenly and obtain the proper shape

2: Using smooth nosed pliers gently compress the lead wire into a flat surface

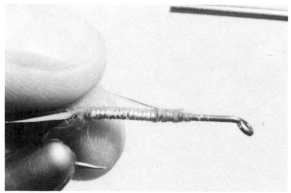

3: Beginning at the front of the fur, mount a long length of flat mono along the side of the body, this is important to ensure a flat, even surface, wrap all the way to the tail and secure tightly

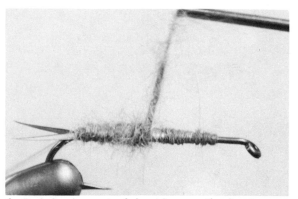

4: Dub body material and wrap the body along the hook into the thorax area

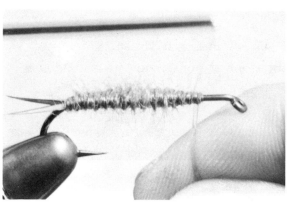

5: Rib the body with the mono keeping an even distance between each wrap, if the above has been done properly the body should have a flat appearance on the top and bottom and a reversed taper toward the rear (large at rear, small in front)

6: Clip off the protruding seal around the body

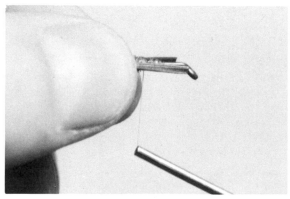

7: Mount goose fibers along the side of the body so they extend to the halfway point

8: Dub on the thorax

9: Mount lacquered duck quill for the thorax and tie it down at the rear of thorax, clip extreme rear into a "V"

10: Dub on a little more fur and build up the thorax

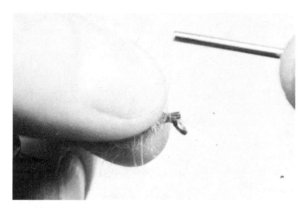

11: Tie down the thorax at the head area

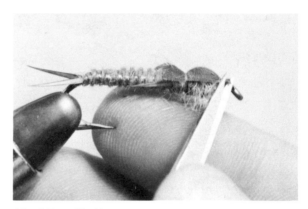

12: Clip off all excess

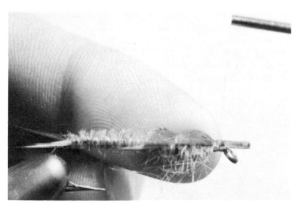

13: Tie in goose fibers along the side of the thorax so they extend to the end of the wingcase

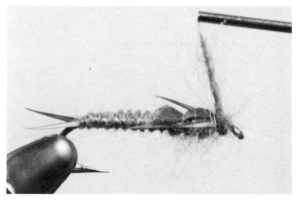

14: Dub on more fur and wrap the head

Part III: Nymph Pattern Dictionary

ATHERTON, DARK (John Atherton)
Hook:	3906B 10-16
Thread:	Black
Tail:	Furnace hackle fibers
Rib:	Oval gold tinsel
Body:	50/50 blend of muskrat and claret seal
Wingcase:	Blue stripped goose
Thorax:	Same as body
Hackle:	2-3 turns of furnace clipped off top and bottom

ATHERTON, LIGHT (John Atherton)
Hook:	3906B 10-16
Thread:	Yellow or white
Tail:	Imitation wood duck
Rib:	Oval gold tinsel
Body:	Cream seal fur
Wing:	Two tiny jungle cock eyes tied over top (optional)
Hackle:	Gray partridge

ATHERTON, MEDIUM (John Atherton)
Hook:	3906B 10-16
Thread:	Brown
Tail:	Brown partridge
Rib:	Oval gold tinsel
Body:	Hare's ear
Wingcase:	Blue stripped goose
Thorax:	Same as body
Hackle:	Brown partridge

BEAVER See p. 38
Hook:	3906B 8-14 weighted
Thread:	Brown
Tail:	Gray partridge fibers
Rib:	Gold wire
Body:	Beaver
Beard Hackle:	Gray partridge fibers

BEGINNERS
Hook:	3906B 10-14
Thread:	Black
Tail:	Bronze mallard or ringneck tail fibers
Rib:	Copper wire
Body:	Muskrat mixed 50/50 with claret seal
Wingcase:	Same as tail
Thorax:	Same as body
Beard Hackle:	Same as tail

BIG HOLE DEMON
Hook:	9672 2-10
Thread:	Black
Tail:	Badger hackle fibers
Body:	Flat silver tinsel
Thorax:	Black chenille palmered with badger hackle
Note:	Furnace hackle may be used in place of badger

BIG STONE NYMPH (Doug Prince)
Hook:	9671, 9672 6-10
Thread:	Black or brown
Tail:	Javalina, 2 quills tied in a "V"
Body:	Brown javalina quills
Wingcase:	Mottled brown turkey
Thorax:	Peacock herl
Hackle:	Dark brown with several turns

---

clipped top and bottom

BIRD'S STONE FLY, BROWN See p. 61
Hook:	9672 4-10 weighted
Thread:	Orange
Tail:	Brown stripped goose tied in a "V"
Rib:	Orange thread
Body:	Beaver or mohlon tied with "twist" method
Wingcase:	Turkey quill
Thorax:	Peacock herl palmered with 3-4 turns of brown saddle hackle

BIRD'S STONE FLY, GRAY (SALMON FLY)
Weighted
Hook:	9672, 9575 4-10
Thread:	Yellow
Tail:	Gray stripped goose tied short and in a "V"
Rib:	Yellow nymo or floss, or silk thread
Body:	Dubbed muskrat or gray mohlon tied with the "twist" method
Wingcase:	Strip of clear plastic
Thorax:	Peacock herl palmered with 3-4 turns of blue dun saddle hackle

BITCH CREEK See p. 54
Hook:	9672, 79580 2-8 weighted
Thread:	Black
Tail:	2 white rubber legs
Body:	Black chenille with strip of orange chenille pulled underneath the body and secured by crisscrossing the thread back over the body
Thorax:	Black chenille palmered with 3-4 turns of brown saddle hackle
Feelers:	Same as tail

BLACK CADDIS EMERGER See p. 70
Hook:	3906B 10-16
Thread:	Black
Tail:	3 moose body hair fibers (black) tied short (tail optional but adds stability)
Body:	"Twisted" black mohlon or rabbit
Thorax:	Black rabbit palmered with black hackle clipped short on top and to the gap of hook on bottom
Wingcase:	Lacquered black duck wing segment clipped to form a sharp "V" on the top and along sides

---

BLACK CREEPER Weighted
Hook:	7959B, 7957BX 8-12
Thread:	Black
Tail:	Black hackle fibers
Rib:	Flat gold tinsel
Body:	Flatten lead wire and cover with black floss, applying lacquer liberally before and while tying the body; flatten again upon completion of the body
Feelers:	Tie a nice bunch of black hackle fibers at right angles, and clip to about 3/4 the length of the body

---

BLACK FORKED TAIL (PRINCE NYMPH)
(Doug Prince)
Hook:	9671, 9672 2-12
Thread:	Black
Tail:	Black stripped goose tied along sides of hook in a "V"
Rib:	Flat or oval silver tinsel
Body:	Black ostrich
Hackle:	Black, 2-4 turns
Wing:	White stripped goose tied over the top of the body in a "V" with goose tips flared up

BLACK HELGRAMITE (Doug Prince) See p. 43
Hook:	3665A, 79580, 9672 6-10 weighted
Thread:	Black
Tail:	Black stripped goose tied short and slightly down in a "V"
Rib:	Optional
Body:	Black floss, mohlon or yarn
Wingcase:	Gray or black goose wing quill or swiss straw
Thorax:	Black rabbit palmered with 3-4 turns black saddle hackle with strip of red wool along the underbody
Legs:	Black stripped goose fibers tied along the sides of the body with tips flaring out and extending about half the length of the body

BLACK MARTINEZ (Don Martinez) See p. 57
Hook:	3906B 8-14
Thread:	Black
Tail:	Few guinea fibers
Rib:	Oval gold tinsel
Body:	Black seal
Wingcase:	Stripped green goose
Thorax:	Black chenille
Hackle:	Mallard flank

BLACK SEAL
Hook:	3906B 10-14
Thread:	Black
Tail:	Black stripped goose tied in a "V"
Rib:	Gold wire
Body:	Black seal
Hackle:	2-3 turns black, clipped off on top

BLADES OLIVE
Hook:	9671, 9672 12-16
Thread:	Olive or black
Tail:	Blue dun hackle fibers
Rib:	Flat gold tinsel
Body:	Golden olive seal
Wingcase:	Orange goose or duck quill feather segment
Hackle:	Creamy badger

BLONDE BURLAP (Polly Rosborough)
Hook:	7957BX 8-12
Thread:	Cream or tan
Tail:	Ginger hackle fibers or tips
Body:	Burlap or blonde sand mohlon depicting segmented look
Hackle:	Light ginger or honey dun
Head:	Referring to the thread part—it

should be long and nicely tapered

BLUE WING OLIVE (Swisher-Richards)
Hook:	94840, 94842 14-24
Thread:	Black
Tail:	Olive mallard or dyed partridge
Body:	Olive and brown rabbit mixed 50/50
Thorax:	Same as body
Wing:	Bunch of black ostrich clipped short
Beard Hackle:	Olive mallard

BOW TIE BUZZER (Frank Sawyer)
Hook:	3906B 12-14
Thread:	Copper wire
Tail:	4 ringneck tail fibers tied very short
Underbody:	Silver mylar or silver tinsel
Body, Wingcase and Thorax:	Ringneck tail fibers. Twist ringneck tail fibers around copper wire and wrap to head, take a couple of extra turns to slightly build up the thorax, wrap to head and fold the remaining tips back over the top of the thorax to form the wingcase, secure with wire

BREADCRUST
Hook:	3906, 3906B 10-16
Thread:	Black or orange
Rib:	Gold wire
Underbody:	Orange rabbit and orange seal mixed 50/50
Overbody:	Stripped peacock herl will do, but the original calls for the brown quill from the butt of a dark brown saddle hackle; quill must be flat and have a dark line on shiny side
Hackle:	2 turns of soft grizzly

BROWN AND OLIVE
Hook:	3906B 12-16
Thread:	Black
Tail:	Peacock sword
Rib:	Oval gold tinsel
Body:	Olive yarn or fur
Thorax:1	Peacock herl
Hackle:	2-3 turns of furnace

BROWN BOMBER Weighted
Hook:	3906, 3906B 10-14
Thread:	Black or gray
Rib:	Flat gold tinsel
Body:	Muskrat
Hackle:	Brown partridge

BROWN DRAKE (Al Troth)
Hook:	9672 8-12
Thread:	Yellow
Tail:	Gray brown marabou tied short
Body:	Gold rabbit painted black along sides with black felt marking pen
Wing:	Gray brown marabou tied in after body; should extend the length of the body
Wingcase:	Gray goose quill segment
Thorax:	Gold rabbit
Hackle:	Brown partirdge along sides of body and underneath body
Head:	Gold rabbit

BROWN DRAKE, DARK (Randall Kaufmann)
Hook:	7957BX 8-12
Thread:	Black or tobacco brown
Tail:	2 dark brown javalina quills
Body:	Dark brown rabbit, painted black on top with felt marking pen

Wingcase:	Dark ringneck pheasant tail fibers painted as per body
Thorax:	Same as body
Hackle:	Dyed brown partridge tied along sides

BROWN FORKED TAIL (Doug Prince) See p. 59
Hook:	9671, 9672 4-12 weighted
Thread:	Black
Tail:	Brown stripped goose tied in a "V" and not too long
Rib:	Flat gold tinsel
Body:	Peacock herl
Hackle:	2-4 turns dark brown
Wing:	White stripped goose tied in a "V" over the top of the body so the tips flare up

BROWN SCUD See p. 32
Hook:	7957X 8-16 slightly weighted
Tail:	Brown hackle fibers tied short
Shellback:	Clear plastic strip
Rib:	Copper wire
Body:	Mixture of 75% brown seal and 25% brown rabbit
Beard hackle:	Optional, brown hackle fibers

BURKE
Hook:	3906B 10-16
Thread:	Black
Body:	Horse mane—brown or black
Thorax:	Black chenille or rabbit with 3 turns of palmered furnace hackle

BURLAP
Hook:	7957BX 6-12
Thread:	Brown
Tail:	Moose, deer, or elk
Body:	Burlap
Hackle:	2-4 turns of undersized grizzly

CADDIS CASE
Hook:	7957BX, 6-14
Thread:	Black
Body:	Fur underbody; after completing the underbody apply epoxy, plio bond, or other suitable glue, place in small box of fine to medium gravel and shake, let dry

CADDIS EMERGER (Randall Kaufmann)
Hook:	3906B, 7957BX 6-14
Thread:	Black
Tail:	3 moose body hair fibers
Rib:	Copper wire
Body:	"Twisted" mohlon in gold, yellow, browns, gray or olive
Wing:	Hare's ear fur with guard hair
Head:	2-3 turns gray ostrich and peacock

CADDIS LARVA
Hook:	3906B 8-14
Thread:	Black
Body:	Tan chenille
Thorax:	Black chenille
Hackle:	2-3 turns brown

CADDIS PUPA
Hook:	7957BX, 3906B 10-18
Thread:	Black
Body:	Rabbit and seal mixed 50-50; can be almost any natural color, with brown and grays being the best
Beard Hackle:	Brown Partridge (tied in before head)

Head:	Same as body

CAREY SPECIAL (Tom Carey) See p. 73
Hook:	9761, 9672 6-14
Thread:	Black
Tail:	Ringneck rump or tail fibers
Rib:	Any color fine wire
Body:	Can be almost anything; peacock, ringneck tail fibers, wool, floss, etc.
Hackle:	Same as tail, tied full and long

CARROT See p. 34
Hook:	3906B 10-16
Thread:	Orange mono or nymo
Tail:	Black hackle fibers
Body:	Orange thread
Thorax:	Black chenille or fur
Hackle:	2-3 turns of black

CASUAL DRESS (Polly Rosborough)
Hook:	9672, 79580, 1206 2-10
Thread:	Black
Tail:	Muskrat with guard hairs
Body:	Muskrat fur "segmented" look (twist method or noodle)
Collar:	Muskrat fur with guard hair
Head:	Black ostrich herl

CATE'S TURKEY (Jerry Cate) See p. 40
Hook:	94840 14-16
Thread:	Black
Tail:	A few wisps of mallard fibers dyed wood duck color
Rib:	Gold wire (rib complete fly)
Body:	Section of dark mottled turkey quill
Head:	2-3 turns peacock herl
Beard Hackle:	Few wisps mallard dyed wood duck

COLORADO CADDIS
Hook:	9671 or "Flymph" hook 8-12
Thread:	Yellow
Shellback:	Gray goose
Rib:	Yellow silk (optional)
Body:	Light yellow mohlon
Hackle:	2-3 turns black
Antennae:	6-10 black hackle fibers extending straight out and slightly up from the eye of the hook

CREAM
Hook:	3906B, 7947BX 10-14
Thread:	Cream or yellow
Tail:	Mallard dyed wood duck
Body:	Cream chenille
Wingcase:	Mallard dyed wood duck
Thorax:	Cream chenille palmered with 3 turns of cream hackle

CRESS BUG
Hook:	3906 8-14
Thread:	Gray
Body:	Mixture 25% muskrat, 75% gray seal, trim top close and taper the sides and underbody, paint black strip over the top with black felt marking pen

DANDY GREEN
Hook:	3906B, 7957BX 6-10
Thread:	Olive

Tail: Greenish gray ringneck body feathers

Body: Mixture of 50% olive rabbit, 20% yellow rabbit, 10% yellow seal, 20% light green seal, and 10% dark green seal

Hackle: Same as tail

DARK GREEN DRAKE (Al Troth)

Hook: 3906B 8-12
Thread: Olive
Tail: 3 moose body hair fibers
Rib: Heavy dark brown silk thread
Body: Dark olive rabbit
Wingcase: Black duck quill segment
Thorax: Same as body
Hackle: Dark olive partridge or mallard

DARK HENDRICKSON

Hook: 3906B 10-16
Thread: Black
Tail: Blue dun hackle fibers
Body: Stripped peacock herl with underbody built up with brown fur
Wing: Gray duck shoulder 1/3 body length
Beard Hackle: Blue dun hackle fibers

DARK HENDRICKSON

Hook: 3906B 12-16
Thread: Red
Tail: Tips of two black and one brown moose mane
Body: Underbody brown fur or floss, overbody two black and one brown moose mane strands tied in at the tips
Wing: Gray duck shoulder feather 1/3 the length of the body
Hackle: Rusty dark blue dun clipped on top

DARK HENDRICKSON (Al Troth)

Hook: 3906B 8-12
Thread: Brown
Tail: 3 moose body hair fibers
Body: Dark brown ostrich with overlay of dark brown javalina
Wingcase: Black duck quill segment
Thorax: Dark brown rabbit
Hackle: Dyed brown partridge or suitable substitute

DAVIS LAKE

Hook: 3906B 8-12
Thread: Brown
Body: Cream fur or mohlon, wool, etc.
Feelers: Small bunch of brown hackle fibers tied in such a manner that they are pointing nearly straight up and slightly forward over the eye of the hook

DOMINO (Hank Roberts)

Hook: 9671 8-12
Thread: Black
Tail: Black hackle fibers
Ribbing: Black saddle hackle "pulled off" on top and clipped to 1/8-1/4" sides and bottom
Body: Woven floss, white under, black top 1/3 length of hook
Thorax: 2/3 length of hook, or twice the length of the body—build up underbody with floss or fur so largest portion is in center of hook,

with the taper sloping down toward the eye of the hook, color same as body
Hackle: Black, clipped short on top
Feelers: Gray stripped goose, fine fibers pointing forward from eye

DRAGON

Hook: 9671 8-12
Thread: Black
Body: Olive chenille
Wing: Section of jungle fowl hackle (black with white center and tips) with tip clipped out to form a "V" at end of feather, wing should extend the length of the body, may substitute mallard, seal, or light partridge for jungle fowl hackle
Hackle: Natural dark blue dun—natural or dyed black

DR. WINTER'S

Hook: 9671, 3906B 8-12
Thread: Black
Shellback: 3-4 black ostrich fibers
Body: Peacock herl
Rib: Silver wire
Beard hackle: Black hackle fibers

DUN VARIANT—ISONYCHIA

Hook: 3906B 10-16
Thread: Red or olive
Tail: 3-6 peacock fibers cut short
Body: Black fur mixed with an even amount of claret seal fur
Hackle: Brown partridge

DUSTER (Doug Prince)

Hook: 3906 10-16
Thread: Black
Tail: Black hackle fibers tied sparse
Body: Gray dun ostrich, tie in at tips and twist, wrap body and clip excess ostrich tips to 1/8" over the top of the body
Hackle: 2-3 turns of black clipped off on top

ED BURKE (Ed Burke)

Hook: 3906, 3906B 10-14
Thread: Black
Tail: Black hackle fibers or gray goose
Rib: Oval gold tinsel
Body: Black yarn, mohlon, or fur
Thorax: Black fur
Hackle: 2-3 turns of black

EMERGENT MOSQUITO (Randall Kaufmann)

See p. 39

Hook: 3906 12-18
Thread: Black
Tail: Three short fibers of black moose body hair
Body: Stripped peacock herl over slight taper of dark fur
Thorax: Peacock herl
Wings: Two grizzly hackle tips tied short over top of thorax

EMERGER, BROWN (Swisher-Richards)

Hook: 94840, 3906 10-18
Thread: Brown
Tail: Brown partridge
Rib: Henna (brown) nymo or brown silk thread (rib is optional)
Body: Medium brown rabbit
Wings: Blue dun hen hackle tips
Beard Hackle: Brown partridge

EMERGER, OLIVE (Swisher-Richards)

Hook: 94840, 3906 10-18
Thread: Olive
Tail: Brown partridge
Rib: Olive or green thread (optional)
Body: Olive rabbit
Wing: Blue dun hen hackle tips
Beard Hackle: Brown partridge

EMERGING MARCH BROWN (Al Troth)

Hook: 3906B 10-14
Thread: Brown
Tail: 3 ringneck tail fibers ½-¾" long
Rib: Gold buttonhole twist Cortecelli silk thread
Body: Hare's ear
Thorax: Hare's ear
Collar: Hare's ear tied the length of the body
Wing: Clump of dark brown partridge the length of the collar
Head: Hare's ear

FIRE FLY (Doug Prince)

Hook: 94840 8-14
Thread: Black
Tail: Lady amhurst tippets
Body: 3 part Royal Coachman style body but tied with dyed black peacock herl and fluorescent green floss for center
Hackle: Black
Wing: White stripped goose tied in a "V" over the top of the body with tips pointing up

FISH FLY LARVA

Hook: 9672, 7957 BX 4-8
Thread: Black
Body: Black rabbit mixed with black seal palmered with soft black hackle and clipped to taper (larger at front)
Hackle: Several turns of black hackle slipped to blend with palmered hackle taper

FIZZLE

Hook: 3906, 3906B 8-14
Thread: Black
Shellback: 3-6 peacock fibers
Rib: Heavy black thread or gold wire
Body: Yellow floss
Hackle: Badger—about 3 turns

FLEDERMAUS or BAT FLY

Hook: 3906, 9671, 7957BX 2-12
Thread: Black
Body: Muskrat fur, Heavy body with guard hairs picked out
Wing: Gray squirrel tied slightly shorter than body with hair well spread over the top of the body

FLEDERMAUS (Polly Rosborough)

Hook: 38941, 1206 2-16
Thread: Brown
Body: Muskrat or beaver mixed with brown mink and 10% jackrabbit back
Collar: Muskrat
Wing: Natural teal overlaid with barred brown widgeon extending ¾ of the body length

GIANT BLACK

Hook: 79580, 9575 2-8
Hook: 79580 1-8
Thread: Black
Tail: Dark brown or black stripped goose tied in a "V"

Body: Mixture of: 40% black rabbit, 20% iron blue seal fur, 20% brown rabbit, 20% black seal

Wingcase: Mottled dark brown turkey or speckled hen quill; there are two sections of wingcase, and they are tied as a "wing" with one being tied in the middle of the thorax and the other at the front of the thorax

Thorax: Same as body
Hackle: Black
Head: Same as body
Antennae: Two goose fibers same color as tail

GIANT SALMON FLY, Weighted (Ernest Schwiebert)

Hook: 79580, 1206 1-8
Thread: Brown
Tail: Dark brown stripped goose tied short in a "V"
Body: Brown flat monofilament over flattened black floss with the underbody painted orange
Thorax: Same as body
Wingcase: Dark brown goose (should be 2-3 tied in flat over body at the rear, middle and front of thorax)
Legs: Dyed dark brown ringneck body feather
Antennae: Same as tail

GINGER QUILL (Hank Roberts)

Hook: 9671 8-12
Thread: Black
Tail: Brown hackle fibers
Rib: Brown hackle
Body: Woven floss, beige underneath and dark brown on top
Thorax: Same as body
Hackle: Grizzly along the sides and underneath (clip off on top)
Feelers: Gray stripped goose fibers
Note: See Domino for proportions and instructions before tying

GOLDEN QUILL

Hook: 3906B 10-16
Thread: Yellow
Tail: Stripped gray goose tied short in a "V"
Rib: Gold wire
Body: Stripped stem of a gray duck quill wrapped over yellow floss
Hackle: Brown partridge

GOLDEN SPRING (Randall Kaufmann)

Hook: 9672, 79580 4-8 weighted
Tail: Brown stripped goose tied in a "V"
Rib: Gold thread
Body: Gold mohlon tied with the twist method
Wingcase: Gold turkey
Thorax: Peacock herl palmered with 3-4 turns of brown saddle hackle

GOLDEN STONE (Polly Rosborough)

Hook: 1206 4-6
Thread: Antique gold Belding silk
Tail: Teal dyed gold
Shellback: Teal dyed gold
Rib: Antique gold Cortecelli silk
Body: Gold mohlon
Wings: Gold teal 1/3 body length
Legs: Gold teal

GRANDE STONE

Hook: 9672 6-10

Thread: Gray
Tail: Brown hackle fibers, stripped goose, or 2 brown hackle stems tied in a "V"
Rib: Oval gold tinsel
Body: Gray wool, mohlon, or muskrat
Wingcase: Brown mottled turkey
Thorax: Muskrat with 3-4 turns of palmered brown hackle
Feelers: Turkey (when pulling over wingcase do not clip off all the excess but divide leftovers, forming 2 feelers 1/3' long)

GRANNOM

Hook: 3906B 10-14
Thread: Brown
Body: Mixture of dark brown rabbit and brown seal—about 50/50
Rib: Copper wire
Wingcase: Natural gray duck quill sections tied along the sides extending half the length of the body
Beard Hackle: Brown partridge tied in after the wingcase and before thorax
Thorax: Same as body

GRAY Weighted

Hook: 9672 6-14
Thread: Gray
Tail: Grizzly hackle fibers
Body: Muskrat
Hackle: 2-3 turns grizzly hackle

GRAY CADDIS

Hook: 3906B 10-14
Thread: Black
Body: Gray mohlon or wool
Wings: Two black hackle tips extending along the sides of the body to the bend of the hook
Head: Peacock herl

GRAY DRAKE (Swisher-Richards)

Hook: 3906, 3906B, 7957BX 8-14
Thread: Gray
Tail: Grown partridge
Body: Gray muskrat fur (may mix in a little gray seal for more action and translucence when wet)
Wingcase: Dark gray duck quill segment
Thorax: Same as body
Legs: Brown partridge

GRAY FOX

Hook: 3906B 10-16
Thread: Gray
Tail: Grizzly hackle fibers
Body: 50/50 mixture of cream seal and cream rabbit
Wingcase: Mallard
Thorax: Same as body
Beard hackle: Light partridge

GRAY RAT (Doug Prince)

Hook: 3906, 7957BX 6-12
Thread: Black
Tail: Light dun gray hackle fibers tied short
Body: Muskrat—picked out so the body is fuzzy
Hackle: 2-4 turns light gray dun hackle

GREEN CADDIS

Hook: 3906B 14-16
Thread: Blkack
Body: Fluorescent green fuzzy wool
Wing: Gray duck shoulder feathers clipped to point and placed along both sides of the body

---

Beard Hackle: Blue dun hackle fibers
Head: 2-3 turns black ostrich

GREEN DAMSEL

Hook: 9672 6-10
Thread: Black
Tail: 2 brown hackle tips length of body
Rib: Flat or oval gold tinsel
Body: Olive yellow floss
Wingcase: Brown turkey
Thorax: Olive chenille or fur
Legs: Brown partridge fibers extending along the sides of the body

GREEN DAMSEL (Polly Rosborough)

Hook: 79580, 9575 2-8
Hook: 79580 1-8
Thread: Green Belding No. 9550
Tail: Fluff of olive marabou tied short to ¼''
Rib: Green Belding No. 9550
Body: Olive fur or yarn the same color as Belding No. 9550
Wing: Olive marabou about 1/3 the body length

GREEN DRAKE Weighted (Swisher-Richards)

Hook: 3906, 3906B 8-14
Thread: Black
Tail: Brown partridge
Body: Blackish brown mole fur (can also use mixture of rabbit and seal fur)
Wingcase: Black duck quill section
Thorax: Same as body
Legs: Brown partridge

GREEN MOUNTAIN DAMSEL (Randall Kaufmann) See p. 55

Hook: 9672 4-8
Thread: Olive
Tail: Olive stripped goose tied short in a "V"
Shellback: Olive marabou
Rib: Gold wire
Body: Dark green seal
Wing: Olive marabou tied to 1/3 the length of the body

GREEN ROCKWORM (Polly Rosborough)

Hook: 38941, 1206 8-10
Thread: Black
Rib: Dark green thread
Body: Spray green mohlon
Beard Hackle: Dark green guinea
Head: Black ostrich

GREENWELL'S GLORY

Hook: 3906, 94840 8-14
Thread: Olive
Tail: Light brown hackle fibers
Shellback: Mallard flank
Rib: Gold wire
Body: Light olive floss
Hackle: 2-3 turns of furnace or brown

GUNNY SACK

Hook: 9671 8-14
Thread: Black or brown
Tail: Grizzly hackle fibers
Body: Natural burlap palmered with grizzly hackle and clipped short all around

HALFBACK

Hook: 9672 6-12
Thread: Olive
Tail: Brown hackle fibers
Rib: Gold wire
Body: Peacock herl
Thorax: Peacock (wire rib)
Wing: Bunch of brown partridge 1/3 of the body length
Beard Hackle: Brown hackle fibers

HARE'S EAR, GOLD RIBBED See p. 69

Hook: 3906B 8-16 weighted
Thread: Brown
Tail: Hare's ear, taken from ears or mask and tied short

Rib: Oval gold tinsel
Body: Blended hare's ear
Wingcase: Mottled brown turkey
Thorax: Blended hare's ear picked out to suggest legs

HELGRAMITE (Doug Prince) Weighted

Hook: 3665 A, 79580, 9672, 1206 6-10
Thread: Black
Tail: Black stripped goose tied short in a "V"
Rib: Black ostrich, clipped closely all around
Body: Black floss
Wingcase: Gray or black goose section
Thorax: Black rabbit palmered with black saddle hackle with a strip of red wood along the underbody
Legs: Black stripped goose fibers tied along the sides of the body with tips flaring out and extending about ½ the length of the body

HENDRICKSON

Hook: 3906, 3906B 10-14
Thread: Olive
Tail: Mallard dyed wood duck
Rib: Gold wire
Body: 50/50 blend of tan and gray fox fur and claret seal
Wingcase: Gray duck quill
Thorax: Same as body
Hackle: Gray partridge fibers

HENDRICKSON

Hook: 3906B 12-16
Thread: Black
Tail: Bronze mallard—3 fibers
Body: "Twisted" red-brown fur, rabbit being the best
Thorax: Red-brown fur picked out
Wing: Red-brown fur

HENDRICKSON (Art Flick)

Hook: 3906B 10-16
Thread: Olive
Tail: Mallard dyed wood duck
Rib: Gold wire
Body: Even mixture of beaver, muskrat and claret seal fur
Wingcase: Gray goose
Thorax: Same as body
Beard Hackle: Brown partridge

HENRY'S LAKE, DARK

Hook: 3906B, 9671, 7957BX 6-14
Thread: Black
Shellback: Black squirrel pulled over the body and divided at the head to form feelers; shellback should be quite heavy
Body: Yellow chenille

HENRY'S LAKE, LIGHT

Hook: 3906B, 7957BX 6-10
Thread: Black
Tail: Gray squirrel
Wingcase: Gray squirrel shellback type tied in at tail, pulled over the back and tied off at the head; next divide the tips to form antennae
Body: Most any color chenille—yellow being the most popular

HOWELL MAYFLY NYMPH

Hook: 7957BX, 9671, 3906B 8-16
Thread: Black, brown or gray
Tail: Ginger or blue dun hackle fibers
Body: Stripped peacock quill (may rib with fine wire for strength)
Thorax: 2-3 ginger or blue dun hackles wrapped and then clipped to approximately 1/8" on the top and bottom

IDA MAY (Charles Brooks)

Hook: 9672 8-10

Thread: Black
Tail: Grizzly hackle fibers dyed dark green
Rib: Peacock herl and gold wire
Body: Black fuzzy wool or mohlon
Hackle: Grizzly dyed dark green, very sparse

IRON BLUE

Hook: 3906B 14-16
Thread: Gray
Tail: Light gray dun hackle fibers
Rib: Gold wire
Body: Muskrat
Thorax: Muskrat (no rib)
Hackle: Light dun gray

IRON BLUE DUN

Hook: 3906B 10-18
Thread: Yellow, black
Rib: Gold wire
Body: Gray goose quill section
Wingcase: Stripped gray goose
Thorax: Same as body

KAUFMANN'S BLACK STONE (Randall Kaufmann)

Hook: 9575 2-10 weighted (flatten wire with pliers)
Thread: Black
Tail: Black stripped goose tied very short
Rib: Black, flat monofilament
Body: Mixture of dark brown seal, claret seal, black seal, purple seal and black rabbit
Wingcase: Dyed black turkey tied in three sections along the top of the thorax and clipped to a "V"
Thorax: Same as body
Antennae: Black stripped goose

KAUFMANN'S BROWN STONE See p. 76 (Randall Kaufmann)

Hook: 9575 2-10 weighted (flatten lead wire with pliers)
Thread: Brown
Tail: Brown stripped goose tied very short
Rib: Dyed dark brown flat monofilament
Body: Mix dark brown seal and dark brown rabbit with a bit of claret, purple, black and orange seal— clip off excess after rib is in place
Wingcase: Mottled turkey tied in three separate sections along the top of the thorax and clipped to a "V" on top
Thorax: Same as body
Antennae: Brown stripped goose

KAUFMANN'S GOLDEN STONE

Hook: 1206 2-10 weighted
Thread: Orange or yellow
Tail: Brown stripped goose tied very short
Rib: Gold flat monofilament
Body: Mixture of 20% orange seal, 10% yellow seal, 35% amber seal, 15% brown seal and 20% tan hare's ear; clip off all the excess after the rib is in place.
Wingcase: Dyed gold turkey tied in three sections along the top of the thorax and clipped to a "V" on top
Thorax: Same as the body
Antennae: Brown stripped goose

KEMP BUG

Hook: 3906B 8-14
Thread: Black
Tail: 3-6 peacock sword fibers
Rib: Gold wire
Body: Peacock herl
Wing: Two grizzly hackle tips flat over the body for 1/3 of the body length
Hackle: 2-3 turns of furnace tied back

KILLER BUG (Frank Sawyer)

Hook: 3906B 10-12
Thread: Copper wire
Body: Light gray mohair; body should have a very slight taper, and most wild mohair fibers should be clipped off; twist mohair around copper wire

LATEX CADDIS

Hook: 7957BX, 37140, 3906B 6-10 weighted
Thread: Black
Body: Latex; color with Pantone marker (build the underbody up to a nice taper and start body back toward bend of the hook)
Head: Black rabbit

LEADWING COACHMAN

Hook: 9671 10-14
Thread: Brown or olive
Tail: Dark brown hackle fibers
Rib: Copper wire
Body: Peacock herl
Wingcase: Bronze mallard or dark brown duck quill
Thorax: Peacock
Hackle: Rusty brown

LEADWING COACHMAN (Al Troth)

Hook: 3906B 8-14
Thread: Black
Tail: 2 peacock fibers cut short to bend of hook with bronze mallard overlay slightly longer than peacock
Body: Peacock with dark brown javalina overlay; lots of peacock fibers should be coming through between javalina wraps
Wingcase: Black duck quill
Thorax: Dark brown beaver or rabbit
Hackle: Bronze mallard or dyed brown partridge tied along sides and as beard hackle

LEIB'S BUG (Don Leib)

Hook: 9672 6-12
Thread: Black
Tail: Brown stripped goose tied short and in a "V"
Rib: Gold wire
Body: Peacock herl palmered with brown saddle hackle and clipped off on top
Legs: Brown stripped goose fiber tied along each side of hook with the points curving in and extending to the end of the body

LIGHT CAHILL

Hook: 3906B 10-16
Thread: Yellow
Tail: Mallard dyed wood duck
Body: Cream fur (albino beaver, albino muskrat, rabbit or nutria)
Wing: Mallard dyed wood duck about 1/3 length of body

Beard Hackle: Cream hackle fibers (Hackle may also be tied full)

LIGHT CREEPER
Hook: 3906B 10-14
Thread: Black
Tail: Gray squirrel
Rib: Flat gold tinsel
Body: Creamish yellow fur
Thorax: Peacock
Legs: Gray squirrel along sides of body

LIGHT OLIVE
Hook: 3906B 10-18
Thread: Olive
Rib: Oval gold tinsel
Body: Light olive rabbit
Wingcase: Olive duck quill segment or stripped goose
Thorax: Olive fur
Hackle: 2-3 turns olive

LINGREN'S BLACK AND YELLOW (Ira Lingren)
Hook: 3906B 10-16
Thread: Black
Tail: Black hackle fibers
Rib: Gold wire through body and thorax
Body: Yellow marabou
Thorax: Peacock
Hackle: 2-3 turns black clipped top and bottom

LINGREN'S DARK MAY (Ira Lingren)
Hook: 3906B, 9671 12-16
Thread: Black
Tail: Black hackle fibers
Rib: Heavy yellow silk thread
Body: Black thread
Thorax: Peacock herl
Hackle: 2-3 turns black clipped top and sides

LINGREN'S INCH WORM (Ira Lingren)
Hook: 3906B 10-16
Thread: Black
Tail: Black hackle fibers
Body: Fluorescent green fuzzy wool palmered with black ostrich herl

LINGREN'S OLIVE (Ira Lingren) See p. 52
Hook: 3906B 10-18
Thread: Black
Tail: Black hackle fibers
Rib: Gold wire
Body: Olive marabou
Thorax: Peacock herl
Hackle: 2-3 turns black hackle clipped top and bottom

LINGREN'S PEACOCK (Ira Lingren)
Hook: 3906B 10-16
Thread: Black
Tail: Black hackle fibers
Rib: Gold wire
Body: Peacock herl
Hackle: 2-3 turns black clipped top and bottom

LINGREN'S WOOD DUCK (Ira Lingren)
Hook: 3906B 10-18
Thread: Black
Tail: Imitation wood duck
Rib: Gold wire
Body: Imitation wood duck
Thorax: Black ostrich
Legs: Few wisps along the sides of the body

LINGREN'S YELLOW (Ira Lingren)
Hook: 3906B 10-16
Thread: Black
Tail: Black hackle fibers
Rib: Gold wire
Body: Yellow marabou
Hackle: 2-3 turns black—clipped top and bottom

LITTLE GRAY CADDIS (Pupa) (Charles Brooks)
Hook: 9671 8-10
Thread: Brown
Tail: Short bright green fuzz as egg sack
Rib: Gold wire
Body: Gray wool, mohlon or fur
Thorax: Gray or tan ostrich
Wing: Gray or tan ostrich clipped to ¼'' (use ends of thorax)
Hackle: Sparse gray or brown partridge

LITTLE RED STONEFLY (Ernest Schwiebert)
Hook: 9671 10-14
Thread: Rusty brown
Tail: Brown stripped goose tied short (or hen hackles)
Body: Reddish brown floss flattened and painted black at lateral margins, over which is wound reddish brown flat monofilament
Thorax: Same as body
Wingcases: Brown mottled speckled hen (tie 2-3 separate sections spaced throughout the thorax)
Legs: Reddish brown hen hackle or speckled hen quill
Antennae: Brown stripped goose tied so they flare out and away from the eye of the hook

LITTLE SAND SEDGE
Hook: 3906B 14-16
Thread: Brown
Body: Mixture of 70% pale yellow rabbit and 30% medium brown rabbit
Wing: Gray section of duck quill tied at sides of body and extending for half the body length
Beard Hackle: Brown partridge tied in before the thorax
Thorax: Hare's ear

LONG TAIL MARCH BROWN See p. 36
Hook: 3906B 8-14 weighted
Thread: Black
Tail: Mallard dyed wood duck 1½ length of body
Shellback: Mottled brown turkey
Rib: Yellow tying thread or floss
Body: Blended hare's ear
Hackle: Brown partridge tied along sides and bottom

MAGGOT
Hook: 3906B 10-16
Thread: Black
Shellback: Ringneck tail fibers
Rib: Copper wire
Body: Pale yellow mohlon
Hackle: 2 turns brown

MARABOU
Hook: 9671, 7957B X 8-14
Thread: Black
Tail: Black hackle fibers
Rib: Copper wire

Body: Brown, gray or black marabou conventionally wrapped
Hackle: Black

MARCH BROWN
Hook: 3906B 12-14
Thread: Black
Tail: Bronze mallard
Body: Brownish gray fox or hare's ear tied with the twist method
Thorax: Medium brown rabbit or fox picked out
Wing: Dark brown mink

MARCH BROWN (AMERICAN)
Hook: 3906B 10-16
Thread: Black
Tail: 3-5 strands of black moose body hair
Rib: Stripped peacock herl
Body: Tobacco brown floss
Wingcase: Mottled turkey
Thorax: Peacock herl palmered with 3-4 turns brown hackle

MARCH BROWN (Art Flick)
Hook: 3906B 12-16
Thread: Brown
Tail: 3 fibers from a ringneck tail feather
Rib: Dark brown silk
Body: Mixture of tan red fox belly fur and amber seal (70-30)
Wingcase: Ringneck tail feather section (dark side showing)
Thorax: Same as body
Hackle: Brown partridge either tied as beard or along sides and bottom— but not the top

MATT'S FUR (Matt Lavell) See p. 47
Hook: 9672, 9671 6-12 weighted
Thread: Brown
Tail: Mallard dyed wood duck
Rib: Oval gold tinsel
Body: 50/50 mixture of otter and cream seal
Wingcase: Same as tail
Thorax: Same as body
Hackle: Leftover tips of wingcase are pulled back along the sides and bottom of the fly; these legs should not extend beyond the point of the hook

MAYFLY
Hook: 3906B 10-16
Thread: Black
Tail: Mallard dyed wood duck
Rib: Gold wire
Body: Stripped peacock
Wingcase: Mallard dyed wood duck
Thorax: Peacock herl
Hackle: Use leftover tips from wingcase, though they should not extend beyond the hook point

MICHIGAN
Hook: 9671 10-14
Thread: Black
Tail: Mallard flank fibers
Body: Stripped grizzly hackle stem
Wingcase: Orange feather or floss
Thorax: Gray muskrat or rabbit
Hackle: 1-2 turns of reddish brown

MICHIGAN MAYFLY

Hook:	9671 2-8
Thread:	Black
Tail:	Small bunch of grizzly hackle fibers—spread out
Rib:	Henna (brown) nymo or dark brown silk thread
Body:	Brown mohlon tied with the twist method
Thorax:	Hare's ear
Wings:	Brown ostrich clipped to 1/3 the body length
Legs:	Few wisps of grizzly hackle fibers tied along side of body

MIDGE

Hook:	94840 14-18
Thread:	Black
Tail:	Black
Body:	Stripped peacock herl
Thorax:	Black hackle clipped top and bottom
Note:	Other color variations are quite popular; keep the body the same and try grizzly, gray, brown or olive for the thorax and tail

MINI MIDGE PUPA

Hook:	94842 20-26
Thread:	Black, or size 15/0 white ultra midge
Body:	Stripped peacock
Thorax:	Either brown, black, olive or gray fur

MINK (Doug Prince)

Hook:	7957BX, 3906 6-12
Thread:	Black
Tail:	Brown hackle fibers
Body:	Natural brown mink, picked out so body is very fuzzy
Hackle:	Three turns dark brown

MONTANA DAMSEL

Hook:	9672 6-10
Thread:	Olive or black
Tail:	Stripped olive goose
Body:	Olive chenille
Wingcase:	2 strands olive chenille
Thorax:	Orange chenille palmered with 3-4 turns of black saddle hackle

MONTANA STONE   See p. 65

Hook:	9762 6-10 weighted
Thread:	Black
Tail:	Black hackle fibers
Body:	Black chenille
Wingcase:	2 strands black chenille
Thorax:	Yellow chenille palmered with 3 turns black saddle hackle

MONTANA STONE Weighted

Hook:	9672 6-10
Thread:	Black
Tail:	Black hackle fibers
Body:	Black chenille
Wingcase:	2 strands of black chenille
Thorax:	Yellow chenille palmered with 3 turns of black hackle

MOSQUITO LARVA

Hook:	3906 12-18
Thread:	Black
Tail:	Grizzly hackle fibers
Body:	Stripped peacock quill (herl) over tapered underbody of dark fur
Thorax:	Peacock herl
Feelers:	Grizzly hackle fibers protruding nearly straight up and slightly

forward from head, but not very long

MOUNTAIN MAY (Randall Kaufmann)

Hook:	3906B 10-16
Thread:	Black
Tail:	3 short moose body hair fibers
Body:	Brown ostrich overlaid with monofilament
Wingcase:	Speckled hen quill sections or mottled turkey
Thorax:	Mink (pick out guard hairs)

MUSKRAT (Polly Rosborough)

Hook:	38941, 3906B, 1206 8-14
Thread:	Gray
Body:	Gray muskrat
Head:	Black ostrich
Beard Hackle:	Guinea hackle fibers

NEEDLE FLY (Dawn Holbrook)

Hook:	9672 8-10
Thread:	Black
Rib:	Silver wire
Body:	Can be any color or combination of colors; most popular are peacock and silver tinsel
Hackle:	Brown ringneck rump
Head:	3-5 turns of peacock herl

NYERGES (Gil Nyerges)

Hook:	9672, 3665A 8-12
Thread:	Olive
Tail:	Brown hackle fibers
Body:	Dark olive chenille or fur, palmered with brown saddle hackle and clipped off on top

NYLON

Hook:	9671, 7957BX 8-14
Thread:	Black
Underbody:	Can be most anything; peacock, fur, yarns, tinsel, etc.
Body:	Plastic leader material, either clear or colored
Head:	Black ostrich
Beard Hackle:	Optional; black hackle fibers are the most popular

OLIVE Weighted

Hook:	3906B 10-14
Thread:	Black
Body:	Olive wool scoured to create a buggy look

OLIVE SEDGE   See p. 51

Hook:	3906, 3906B 10-16
Thread:	Brown
Body:	Olive rabbit (mix a little green seal for a translucent buggy effect)
Wingcase:	Gray duck quill sections tied along both sides of the body and extending from 1/2 to 3/4 length of body
Beard Hackle:	Brown partridge tied in before thorax
Thorax:	Hare's ear

OREGON STONE

Hook:	9575, 3665A 6-10
Thread:	Black
Tail:	Ringneck tail fibers
Body:	Pale yellow mohlon painted black on top
Wing:	Ringneck tail fibers extending 1/3 the length of the body
Legs:	Ringneck tail fibers protruding at right angles from head and clipped to 1/4"; there should be a

total of 4 legs—two on each side

PALE WATERY

Hook:	3906B 8-14
Thread:	Gray
Tail:	Blue dun hackle fibers
Rib:	Silver wire or fine oval tinsel
Body:	Gray mohlon or fur
Wingcase:	Purple feather or floss
Thorax:	Muskrat
Hackle:	1-2 turns of blue dun

PALE WATERY DUN

Hook:	3906B 12-16
Thread:	Black
Tail:	Pale ginger or olive hackle fibers
Rib:	Copper wire
Body:	Ginger seal fur
Hackle:	1 turn grizzly (grizzly dyed yellow, or grizzly and yellow mixed together)

PARTRIDGE

Hook:	9671, 7957BX 8-14
Thread:	Black
Tail:	Few wisps of ringneck tail fibers
Rib:	Yellow nymo or silk thread
Body:	Blended hare's ear
Hackle:	Partridge, short on top and longer underneath; nothing along the sides

PEACOCK (Doug Prince)

Hook:	3906, 3906B 8-12
Thread:	Black
Tail:	3 stubs of peacock herl spread out and pointing down
Rib:	Gold wire
Body:	Peacock wrapped to within 1/16" of head and closely clipped top and bottom
Thorax:	Large thick peacock herl—not
Hac	clipped
Hackle:	2 turns of black—clipped off on top

PHEASANT TAIL

Hook:	3906B 10-16
Thread:	Black
Tail:	Ringneck body fibers—ginger in color
Rib:	Oval gold tinsel or gold wire
Body:	Same as tail
Hackle:	Same as tail

PHEASANT TAIL (Frank Sawyer)

Hook:	3906B 12-14
Thread:	Copper wire
Tail:	4 tips from a ringneck tail tied very short
Body, Wingcase and Thorax:	Ringneck tail fibers; see Bow Tie Buzzer for tying details

PIG NYMPH (Doug Prince)

Hook:	94840 10-20
Thread:	Black, or color to suit
Tail:	Javalina quill points—natural dark brown
Body:	Javalina quills (split in half for smaller flies) dyed tan, brown, yellow, gray, black or olive
Thorax:	Ostrich herl darker than body color
Hackle:	2-4 turns of natural or dyed hackle, compatible in color with the body and thorax, and clipped off top—or top and bottom on the smaller hook size

PKCK (Dave Powell and Jim Kilburn)

Hook:	3906B, 7957BX 8-16
Thread:	Black
Tag:	Silver tinsel
Rib:	Silver wire over stripped peacock quill
Body:	Medium to dark green wool, mohlon or fur
Wingcase:	Turkey
Thorax:	Brown yarn or fur
Legs:	One strip of black ostrich tied short along sides of body

PUGET BUG (Enos Bradner)

Hook:	3906B, 7957BX 10-12
Thread:	Black
Tail:	Black stripped goose to 1/3" or shorter tied in a "V"
Body:	Moose mane, alternating black and white
Thorax:	Peacock
Hackle:	Gray partridge

PUPA LARVA

Hook:	3906B 10-18
Thread:	Black
Body:	Most any color fur with black, olive, claret, tan, gray, yellow and and brown being the most common
Hackle:	Hackle is tied in before the head and clipped top and bottom
Head:	Black ostrich

PUSSYCAT (Joseph Miotle)

Hook:	9672, 79580 8-10
Thread:	Black or olive
Tail:	Natural greenish ringneck rump feathers
Body:	Muskrat, beaver and olive chenille or poly yarn blended equally
Beard Hackle:	Same as tail
Wing:	Dark mottled ringneck body feather trimmed to 1/3 the body length

QUILL GORDON

Hook:	3906B 12-14
Thread:	Gray, brown or black
Tail:	Mallard dyed wood duck
Body:	Mixture of 70% gray rabbit or muskrat and 30% brown seal
Wingcase:	Black duck wing quill segment
Thorax:	Same as body
Beard Hackle:	Mallard dyed wood duck

QUILL GORDON

Hook:	3906B 12-26
Thread:	Gray
Tail:	Mallard dyed wood duck
Body:	Tannish gray muskrat
Wing:	Natural mallard flank feather 1/3 the body length
Hackle:	2-3 turns light blue dun clipped on top

QUILL GORDON

Hook:	3906B 12-16
Thread:	Black or gray
Tail:	Bronze mallard
Body:	"Twisted" brownish gray fox or hare's ear
Thorax:	Gray rabbit or muskrat
Wing:	Dark gray rabbit, fox or muskrat

RAGGLE BOMB Weighted

Hook:	3906 10-14
Thread:	Black
Body:	Peacock herl with palmered

brown hackle; with this pattern it is advisable to tie in the hackle tip first; this will create a swept effect with the hackle as all hackle will slant back naturally

RAINBOW

Hook:	3906B, 7957BX 8-14
Thread:	Black
Tail:	Gray squirrel or grizzly hackle fibers
Rib:	Black silk, fairly heavy
Body:	Brown mohlon or fur
Hackle:	Grizzly and black, 1-2 turns undersized

RANDALL'S BROWN DRAGON (Randall Kaufmann)

Hook:	9575 2-8 weighted (flatten lead wire with pliers); see Randall's Green Dragon tying instructions for more detail
Thread:	Black
Tail:	Brown stripped goose tied extremely short
Rib:	Dark brown flat monofilament
Body:	Dark brown seal (clip off excess after the rib is in place)
Legs:	Brown stripped goose
Thorax:	Same as body
Wingcase:	Extremely dark turkey
Head:	Same as body

RANDALL'S CADDIS (Randall Kaufmann)
See p. 72

Hook:	7957BX 6-14 weighted
Thread:	Black
Rib:	Copper wire (rib entire body and thorax)
Body:	Mohlon tied with the "twist" method; popular colors are browns, greens, yellows, gray and black; for a more curved effect, start the body back on the hook bend
Thorax:	Peacock and black ostrich wound together
Beard Hackle:	Few wisps of black hackle fibers

RANDALL'S GREEN DRAGON (Randall Kaufmann) See p. 79

Hook:	Eagle Claw 1206 4-8 weighted
Thread:	Olive
Tail:	Olive stripped goose tied in "V" extremely short
Rib:	Clear flat monofilament
Body:	Mixture of 40% olive rabbit and 60% insect green seal (clip short after rib)
Legs:	Olive stripped goose tied at the front of the body extending back along sides of the body to the halfway point with tips curving in toward the body
Thorax:	Same as the body
Wingcase:	Olive duck quill segment tied down at the rear of the thorax and the front with approximately ¼" extending out over the body and clipped to a "V"
Legs:	Olive stripped goose tied in front of the thorax and extending back along the sides to end of the wingcase; tips of the goose should curve in toward the body
Head:	Same as the body

RIFFLE DEVIL (Charles Brooks)

Hook:	1206, 79580 4-6
Thread:	Black

Palmered Hackle: 1 ginger and 1 brown saddle tied in tip first
Body: Large olive chenille

R. K. BROWN (Randall Kaufmann)

Hook:	3906B 10-16
Thread:	Tobacco brown
Tail:	Dyed brown partridge or bronze mallard
Body:	Dark brown rabbit (wrap the body a couple of turns behind the tail)
Wingcase:	Same as tail
Thorax:	Same as body
Legs:	Tie leftover tips of wingcase back along sides of thorax
Head:	Same as body

R. K. CADDIS Weighted (Randall Kaufmann)

Hook:	7957BX 6-14
Thread:	Black
Rib:	Copper wire over body and thorax
Body:	"Twisted" mohlon; best colors are pale yellow, gray, browns, greens and black
Thorax:	Black or gray ostrich wound with peacock herl—2-4 turns
Beard Hackle:	Few wisps of black hackle fibers

R. K. CREAM (Randall Kaufmann)

Hook:	3906B 10-16
Thread:	Yellow
Tail:	Light partridge
Body:	Cream nutria (start the body behind the tail)
Wingcase:	Light partridge
Thorax:	Cream nutria
Legs:	Light partridge
Head:	Cream nutria

R. K. HARE'S EAR (Randall Kaufmann)

Hook:	3906 10-16
Thread:	Tobacco brown
Tail:	Brown partridge
Body:	Blended hare's ear (start the body behind the tail)
Wingcase:	Brown partridge
Thorax:	Same as body
Legs:	Tie leftover tips of wingcase back along the sides of the thorax
Head:	Same as body

R. K. MAYFLY (Randall Kaufmann) See p. 67

Hook:	3906B 10-16 weighted
Thread:	Black or brown
Tail:	3 dark moose body hairs
Rib:	4-10 lb. monofilament (preferably shaded brown, not clear)
Body:	Brown ostrich
Wingcase:	Dark speckled hen or turkey
Thorax:	Brown mink picked out to simulate legs

R. K. OLIVE (Randall Kaufmann)

Hook:	3906B 10-16
Thread:	Olive
Tail:	Olive partridge
Body:	Olive rabbit (wrap body a couple of turns behind the tail; this will stand it up and give a natural appearance to the fly)
Wingcase:	Olive partridge
Thorax:	Olive rabbit
Legs:	Olive partridge (use wingcase tips and tie along the side of the thorax)
Head:	Olive rabbit

R. K. TAN (Randall Kaufmann)

Hook:	3906B 10-16
Thread:	Tobacco brown
Tail:	Dyed tan partridge or bronze mallard
Body:	Tan rabbit (wrap the body a couple of turns behind the tail)
Wingcase:	Same as tail
Thorax:	Same as body
Legs:	Leftover tips from wingcase tied along side of the thorax
Head:	Same as body

ROCK WORM

Hook:	9671 10-14
Thread:	Black or olive
Tail:	Peacock fibers clipped to about ¼"
Body:	Medium green or olive fur
Wing:	4 peacock herl fibers clipped to ½ the body length
Hackle:	2-3 turns of green or olive
Feelers:	2 peacock fibers tied ¼" long

RUBBER LEGS—GIRDLE BUG

Hook:	9671, 9672 6-10
Thread:	Black
Tail:	Two sections of white rubber (rubber legs) clipped to 1/3"
Body:	Black chenille (can also use gray, brown or yellow)
Legs:	Same as tail
Note:	The "legs" are evenly spaced throughout the body and protrude at right angles to the body; wrap on a turn or two of chenille, tie in rubber legs, and repeat the process until you have 3 legs along each side of the body)

SAND FLY (Herb Butler)

Hook:	3906B, 7957BX 8-14
Thread:	Black
Tail:	Short bunch of white marabou
Rib:	Yellow Belding silk thread
Body:	Brown floss or fur
Hackle:	2-3 turns of soft ginger

SCUD, BROWN See p. 32

Hook:	7957BX 8-16 slightly weighted
Tail:	Brown hackle fibers tied short
Shellback:	Clear plastic strip
Rib:	Copper wire or monofilament
Body:	Mixture of 75% brown seal and 25% brown rabbit
Beard Hackle:	Optional; brown hackle fibers

SCUD, GRAY Slightly weighted

Hook:	7957BX 8-16
Thread:	Gray
Tail:	Dun gray hackle fibers tied short
Shellback:	Clear plastic
Rib:	Silver wire
Body:	Gray seal, picked out after the fly is finished
Hackle:	1-2 turns of dun gray hackle tied down as beard

SCUD, OLIVE

Hook:	7957BX 8-16
Thread:	Olive
Tail:	Few short wisps of light olive hackle fibers
Shellback:	Clear plastic
Rib:	Light green or olive thread
Body:	Mixture of 40% light olive seal, 20% insect green seal, 20% gray seal, 20% light olive rabbit, 10% pale yellow rabbit

Hackle:	1-2 turns pale olive hackle tied down as beard
Antennae:	Few wisps of mallard dyed wood duck

SCUD, YELLOW

Hook:	7957BX 8-16
Thread:	Yellow
Tail:	Pale yellow hackle fibers tied whort and sparse
Shellback:	Clear plastic strip
Rib:	Yellow or cream thread
Body:	Mixture of 60% pale yellow fur, 15% olive fur, 10% yellow seal, 15% cream seal (pick out fur after completing fly)
Hackle:	1-2 turns of natural ginger tied down as beard
Antennae:	Few wisps of mallard dyed wood duck

SHOT IN THE DARK (Howard Eskin)

Hook:	9672 6-14
Thread:	Dark brown
Rib:	Gold wire
Body:	Palmered grizzly hackle overwrapped with 4-6 peacock fibers twisted around thread; clip grizzly close to the body
Hackle:	2-3 turns grizzly

SHRIMP (SHELLBACK TYPE) Weighted

Hook:	94840, 3906, 3906B, 7957BX 8-12
Thread:	Black or white
Tail:	Brown hackle fibers tied pointing down on extreme bend of hook
Shellback:	Strip of clear plastic
Rib:	Brown saddle hackle palmered through body and clipped short at head
Body:	Olive, tan, pink, gray mohlon, wool or dubbing

SHRIMP NYMPH, GOLD Slightly Weighted (Dave Whitlock)

Hook:	84838 8-16
Thread:	Yellow
Tail:	Grizzly hackle fibers dyed gold
Shellback:	Mottled brown turkey quill dyed gold
Rib:	Gold wire
Body:	Even mixture of gold, amber, yellow seal and gold rabbit
Thorax:	Same as body; pick out seal guard hairs to give slight impression of thorax, but do not rib

SHRIMP NYMPH, GRAY Slightly Weighted (Dave Whitlock)

Hook:	94838 8-18
Thread:	Gray
Tail:	Short bunch of grizzly, mallard or teal
Shellback:	Turkey qill dyed gray
Rib:	Silver wire
Body:	Mixture of 40% gray fur and 60% gray seal
Thorax:	Same as body; pick out guard hair and do not rib

SHRIMP NYMPH, OLIVE Slightly Weighted (Dave Whitlock)

Hook:	94838 8-16
Thread:	Olive
Tail:	Grizzly hackle fibers dyed olive
Shellback:	Turkey quill dyed olive
Rib:	Gold wire
Body:	Olive seal (a mixture of olive, dark green, black, blue and yel-

	low seal makes a fine dark olive shrimp)
Thorax:	Pick out seal guard hair to give a slight impression of a thorax; do not rib

SOWBUG (Dave Whitlock)

Hook:	3906 12-18
Thread:	Gray
Tail:	Gray stripped goose tied very short
Shellback:	Clear plastic
Rib:	Gold wire
Body:	Mixture of 50% muskrat and 50% gray seal picked out along underbody

SPECKLED SPINNER

Hook:	3906B 14-18
Thread:	Gray
Tail:	3 ringneck tail fibers, tied short
Rib:	Gray thread
Body:	Mixture of 50% light gray muskrat and 50% gray seal
Wingcase:	Speckled hen
Thorax:	Same as body
Beard Hackle:	Brown partridge

SPRUCE

Hook:	9671, 9672 6-10
Thread:	Yellow
Tail:	5-8 peacock fibers cut to 1/3"
Shellback:	Gray goose quill section
Rib:	Heavy black silk thread
Body:	Yellow fur or mohlon
Hackle:	Furnace, 3-4 turns tied back along the sides and bottom

SQUIRREL (Doug Prince)

Hook:	3906, 7957BX 6-12
Thread:	Black
Tail:	Gray squirrel
Body:	Gray squirrel body fur picked out so body is fuzzy
Hackle:	2-4 turns of grizzly

STONEFLY CREEPER (Art Flick)

Hook:	3906B 10-12
Thread:	Yellow
Tail:	Two ringneck tail fibers
Shellback:	Mallard dyed wood duck
Body:	Stripped ginger hackle stem wrapped over with light amber seal, heavier for thorax
Hackle:	Brown partridge along sides and bottom; none on top

STRAWMAN

Hook:	9671, 3906B 10-14
Thread:	Gray, brown
Tail:	Mallard—either natural gray or dyed wood duck
Body:	Spun deer hair clipped with a taper; pale yellow rib is optional
Hackle:	Optional; either light partridge or grizzly
Note:	A popular western variation is to tie the body with palmered hackle and clip to shape

SULPHUR DUN

Hook:	3906B 14-18
Thread:	Yellow
Tail:	Mallard dyed wood duck
Body:	Mixture of 50% brown rabbit, 30% yellow rabbit, 10% orange seal, 10% brown seal
Wingcase:	Mottled turkey
Thorax:	Same as body
Beard Hackle:	Mallard dyed wood duck

SUPER GRAY (Howard Eskin) See p. 63

Hook:	7957BX 2-12
Thread:	Black
Tail:	Mallard dyed wood duck
Shellback:	2-6 strands of peacock
Rib:	Gold wire
Body:	Gray mohlon palmered with grizzly hackle clipped off on top
Wing:	Red (fox) squirrel tail extending about to the bend of the hook

T.D.C. (Richard Thompson)

Hook:	3906B, 9671 8-14
Thread:	Black
Rib:	Flat or oval silver tinsel
Body:	Black chenille
Head:	White ostrich, clipped to ¼" or less

TED'S MAYFLY (Ted Trueblood)

Hook:	7957BX 12-16
Thread:	Black
Tail:	3 short, dark deer hair fibers
Body:	Stripped peacock herl
Wingcase:	Extremely fine deer or fox squirrel pulled over and separated at right angles to form feelers
Thorax:	Omit...only thread shows under the wingcase

TED'S STONEFLY Weighted (Ted Trueblood)

Hook:	9672 6-10
Thread:	Black
Tail:	Black hackle fibers or gray stripped goose fibers tied in a "V"
Body:	Brown chenille, tobacco brown being the standard
Wingcase:	Two strips of brown chenille—same as body
Thorax:	Orange chenille palmered with black saddle hackle

TELLICO See p. 35

Hook:	3906B 8-14 weighted
Thread:	Black
Tail:	3-6 guinea fibers
Shellback:	Ringneck tail fibers
Rib:	Peacock herl (do not rib over shellback, just floss the body)
Body:	Yellow floss
Hackle:	2 turns brown hackle

THISTLE BUG

Hook:	7957BX, 9671, 3906B 6-12
Thread:	Black or yellow
Shellback:	5-8 peacock fibers
Rib:	Oval gold tinsel
Body:	Yellow fur or mohlon
Hackle:	Grizzly tied sparse

THUNDERBERG

Hook:	9671, 9672 2-6
Thread:	Black
Tail:	Black bear to 1/3"
Rib:	Silver, gold or copper wire
Body:	Muskrat or beaver fur, well tapered with guard hairs picked out to form the thorax

TIMBERLINE (Randall Kaufmann) See p. 45

Hook:	3906B 10-18 weighted
Thread:	Brown
Tail:	3 moose body hair fibers tied short
Rib:	Copper wire
Body:	Fur from a hare's ear clipped directly from the ears and not matted, body colors can be varied

matted

Wingcase:	Dark side of a ringneck pheasant tail
Thorax:	Same as body
Legs:	Few ringneck tail fibers along each side of body

TIMBERLINE EMERGER (Randall Kaufmann) See p. 31

Hook:	3906, 3257B 10-14
Thread:	Gray
Tail:	3 black moose body hairs
Body:	Mixture of 30% muskrat and 70% gray seal, other popular colors include tan, brown and olive
Wing:	Grizzly hackle tip tied short
Hackle:	2 turns of brown tied back

TORPEDO Weighted

Hook:	9672 6-10
Thread:	Black
Tail:	2 white rubber sections (rubber hackle or legs)
Body:	Black chenille
Thorax:	Black chenille palmered with black saddle hackle
Feelers:	Same as tail

TROUT SHRIMP (Randall Kaufmann) See p. 49

Hook:	7957BX 14-16 slightly weighted
Thread:	Gray
Tail:	Mallard flank
Shellback:	Mallard flank
Rib:	Silver wire
Body:	50/50 mixture of muskrat and gray seal
Feelers:	Mallard flank

TROUT SHRIMP (BROWN) Slightly Weighted (Randall Kaufmann)

Hook:	7957BX 14-16
Thread:	Brown
Tail:	Bronze mallard tied on extreme bend of hook and very short
Shellback:	Bronze mallard
Rib:	Copper wire
Body:	Matted hare's ear mixed with brown seal (picked out along the underbody to simulate tiny legs)
Feelers:	Bronze mallard; the feelers should be the tips of the wingcase; they should be short and pointing up and out from the fly

TROUT SHRIMP (CREAM) Slightly Weighted (Randall Kaufmann)

Hook:	7957BX 14-16
Thread:	Yellow
Tail:	Mallard dyed wood duck (see Brown Trout Shrimp for details)
Shellback:	Mallard dyed wood duck
Rib:	Gold wire
Body:	Mixture of 20% cream or off-white rabbit, 60% cream seal, 20% light yellow seal, and 10% amber seal
Feelers:	Mallard dyed wood duck

TRUEBLOOD CADDIS Weighted (Ted Trueblood)

Hook:	7957BX, 3906B 8-14
Thread:	Black
Tail:	Insect green floss cut to ¼" or shorter, depending on hook size
Shellback:	3-6 peacock fibers
Rib:	Oval silver tinsel
Body:	Insect green floss
Beard Hackle:	Mallard flank feathers

TRUEBLOOD SHRIMP (Ted Trueblood) See p. 42

Hook:	7957BX, 3906, 3906B 8-16 weighted
Thread:	Brown unweighted, green weighted
Tail:	Brown partridge fibers
Body:	50/50 mixture of otter and natural cream seal
Beard Hackle:	Brown partridge fibers
Note:	Outstanding variations are tied with black rabbit mixed with black seal, or muskrat mixed with gray seal

WATER BUG

Hook:	7957BX 6-10
Thread:	Brown or black
Shellback:	Mallard flank feather fibers
Rib:	Copper wire
Body:	Dark brown mohlon or fur—heavily "scoured"

WATER SWEEP (Randall Kaufmann)

Hook:	7957BX 8-12
Thread:	Black or brown
Tail:	Brown stripped goose tied in a "V"
Shellback:	Ringneck tail fibers
Body:	Hare's ear
Legs:	Brown stripped goose
Note:	Body and wingcase are 2 parts; each part being exactly the same; wrap on the body over the rear half of the hook, pull over wingcase, and tie a section of stripped goose along each side of the body so they point out at right angles to the body; repeat above for the front half of fly

WESTERN GREEN DRAKE

Hook:	3906B 8-12
Thread:	Olive
Tail:	Dyed olive partridge
Body:	Dark brown rabbit
Rib:	Cortecelli olive silk
Wingcase:	Dyed olive partridge
Thorax:	Olive brown rabbit
Legs:	Dyed olive partridge

WHITEFISH

Hook:	3906B, 9671 10-14
Thread:	Black or yellow
Body:	Pale yellow angora or mohlon palmered with brown hackle and clipped to ¼" or shorter

WHIT NYMPH, BLACK Weighted (Dave Whitlock)

Hook:	9575
Thread:	Black
Tail:	6 pound monofilament—dyed dark brown or black
Rib:	Oval silver tinsel
Body:	Mixture of 70% black seal and 30% red, yellow, orange, claret and brown seal
Wingcase:	Peacock herl
Thorax:	Same as body
Hackle:	Very soft brownish black, 2-3 turns tied down as beard
Antennae:	Same as tail
Head:	The rear half of the thread head can be painted red

YELLOW MIDGE PUPA (Al Troth)

Hook:	9671, 9672 8-12
Thread:	Olive

Tail:	Mallard dyed wood duck tied short
Rib:	Peacock herl with overrib of gold wire
Hackle:	Brown
Head:	Olive chenille

ZUG BUG See p. 75

Hook:	3906B 8-14
Thread:	Black
Tail:	306 peacock sword fibers
Rib:	Flat or oval silver tinsel
Body:	Peacock herl
Wing:	Mallard dyed wood duck clipped to 1/3 body length
Beard Hackle:	Brown hackle fibers

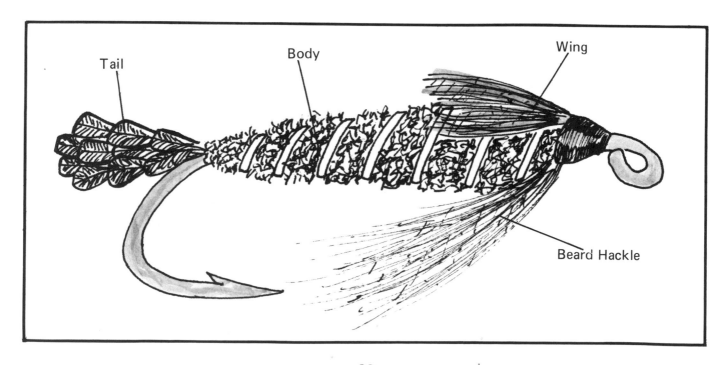

Tail   Body   Wing   Beard Hackle

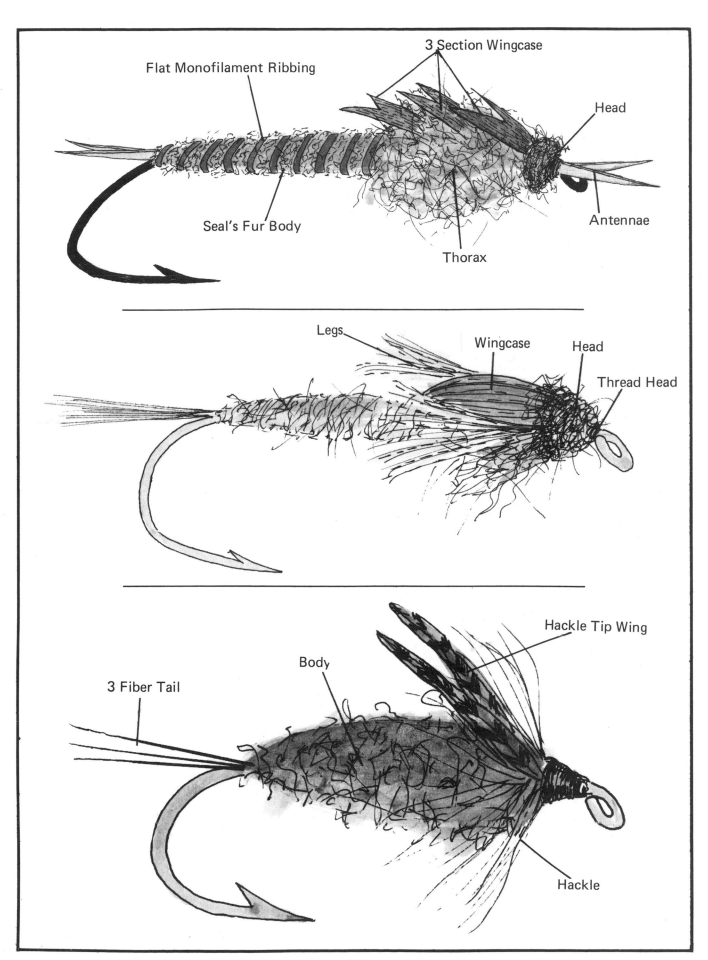

Flat Monofilament Ribbing

3 Section Wingcase

Head

Antennae

Seal's Fur Body

Thorax

Legs

Wingcase

Head

Thread Head

Hackle Tip Wing

Body

3 Fiber Tail

Hackle

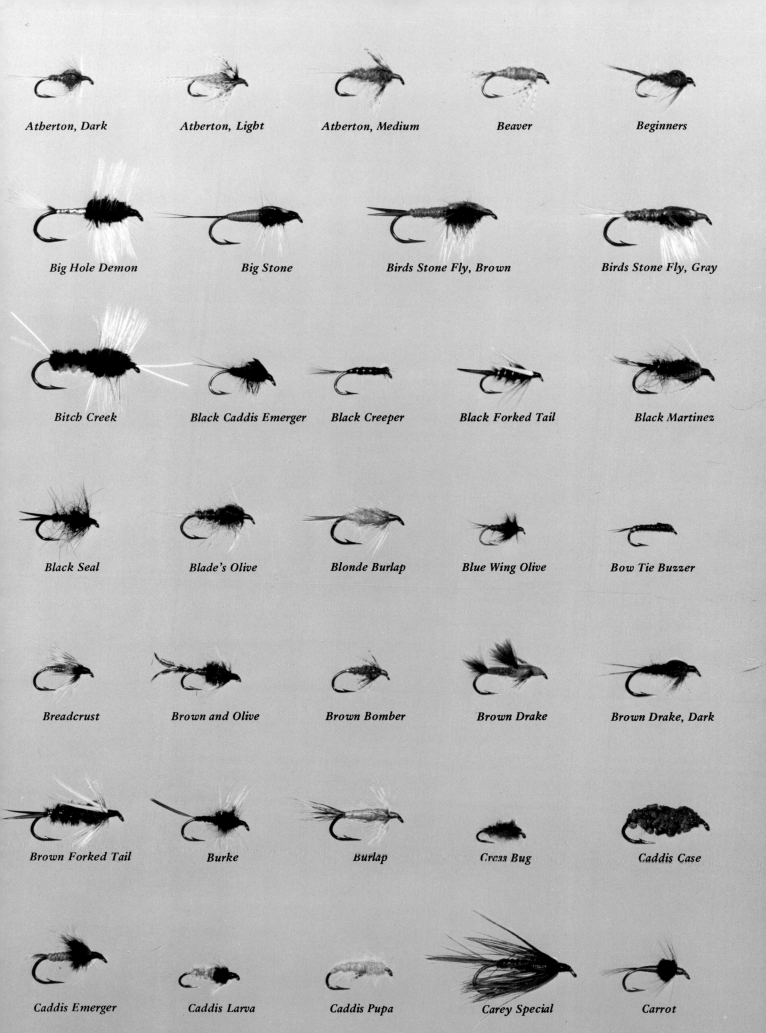

Atherton, Dark

Atherton, Light

Atherton, Medium

Beaver

Beginners

Big Hole Demon

Big Stone

Birds Stone Fly, Brown

Birds Stone Fly, Gray

Bitch Creek

Black Caddis Emerger

Black Creeper

Black Forked Tail

Black Martinez

Black Seal

Blade's Olive

Blonde Burlap

Blue Wing Olive

Bow Tie Buzzer

Breadcrust

Brown and Olive

Brown Bomber

Brown Drake

Brown Drake, Dark

Brown Forked Tail

Burke

Burlap

Cress Bug

Caddis Case

Caddis Emerger

Caddis Larva

Caddis Pupa

Carey Special

Carrot

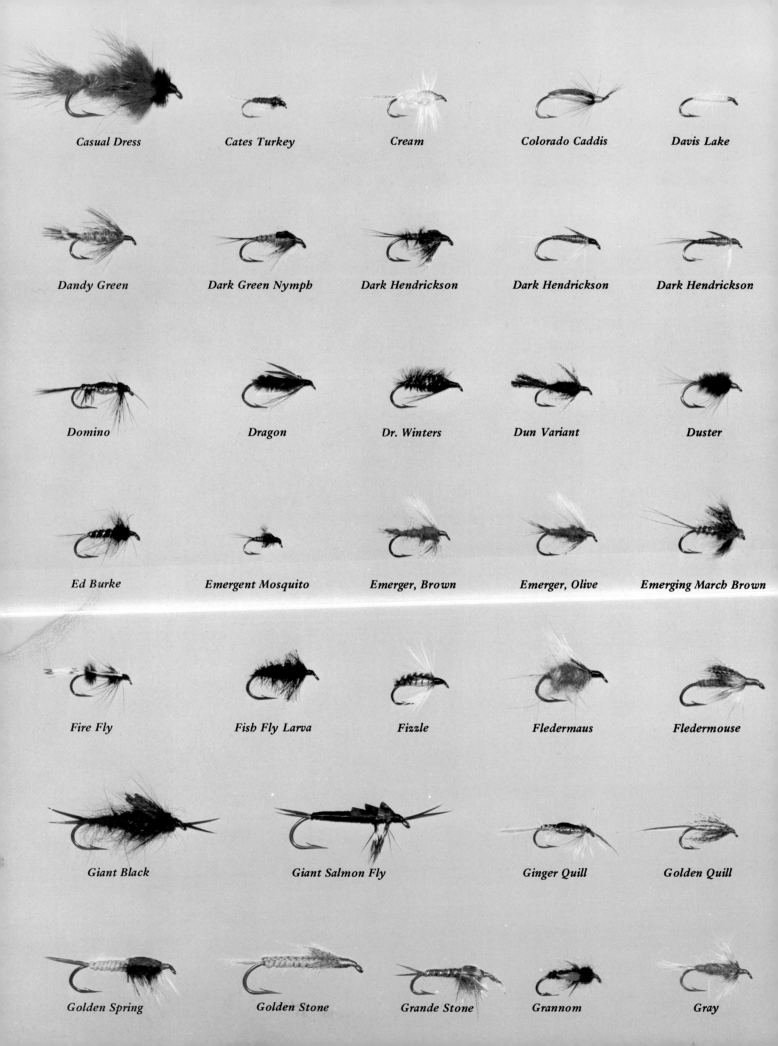

Casual Dress   Cates Turkey   Cream   Colorado Caddis   Davis Lake

Dandy Green   Dark Green Nymph   Dark Hendrickson   Dark Hendrickson   Dark Hendrickson

Domino   Dragon   Dr. Winters   Dun Variant   Duster

Ed Burke   Emergent Mosquito   Emerger, Brown   Emerger, Olive   Emerging March Brown

Fire Fly   Fish Fly Larva   Fizzle   Fledermaus   Fledermouse

Giant Black   Giant Salmon Fly   Ginger Quill   Golden Quill

Golden Spring   Golden Stone   Grande Stone   Grannom   Gray

Gray Caddis

Gray Drake

Gray Fox

Gray Rat

Green Caddis

Green Damsel

Green Damsel

Green Drake

Green Mountain Damsel

Green Rockworm

Greenwell's Glory

Gunney Sack

Halfback

Hare's Ear, Gold Ribbed

Helgramite

Hendrickson

Hendrickson

Hendrickson

Henry's Lake, Dark

Henry's Lake, Light

Howell Mayfly
Nymph, Ginger

Howell Mayfly
Nymph, Dun

Ida May

Iron Blue

Iron Blue Dun

Kaufmann's Black Stone

Kaufmann's Brown Stone

Kaufmann's Golden Stone

Kemp Bug

Killer Bug

Laytex Caddis

Leadwing Coachman

Leadwing Coachman

Leib's Bug

Light Cahill	*Light Creeper*	*Light Olive*	*Lingren's Black and Yellow*	*Lingren's Dark May*
Lingren's Inchworm	*Lingren's Olive*	*Lingren's Peacock*	*Lingren's Wood Duck*	*Lingren's Yellow*
Little Gray Caddis	*Little Red Stonefly*	*Little Sand Sedge*	*Long Tail March Brown*	*Maggot*
Marabou	*March Brown*	*March Brown, American*	*March Brown*	*Matt's Fur*
Mayfly	*Michigan*	*Michigan Mayfly*	*Midge*	*Mink*
Mini Midge Pupa	*Montana Damsel*	*Montana Stone*	*Mosquito Larva*	*Mountain May*
Muskrat	*Needle Fly*	*Nyerges*	*Nylon*	*Olive*

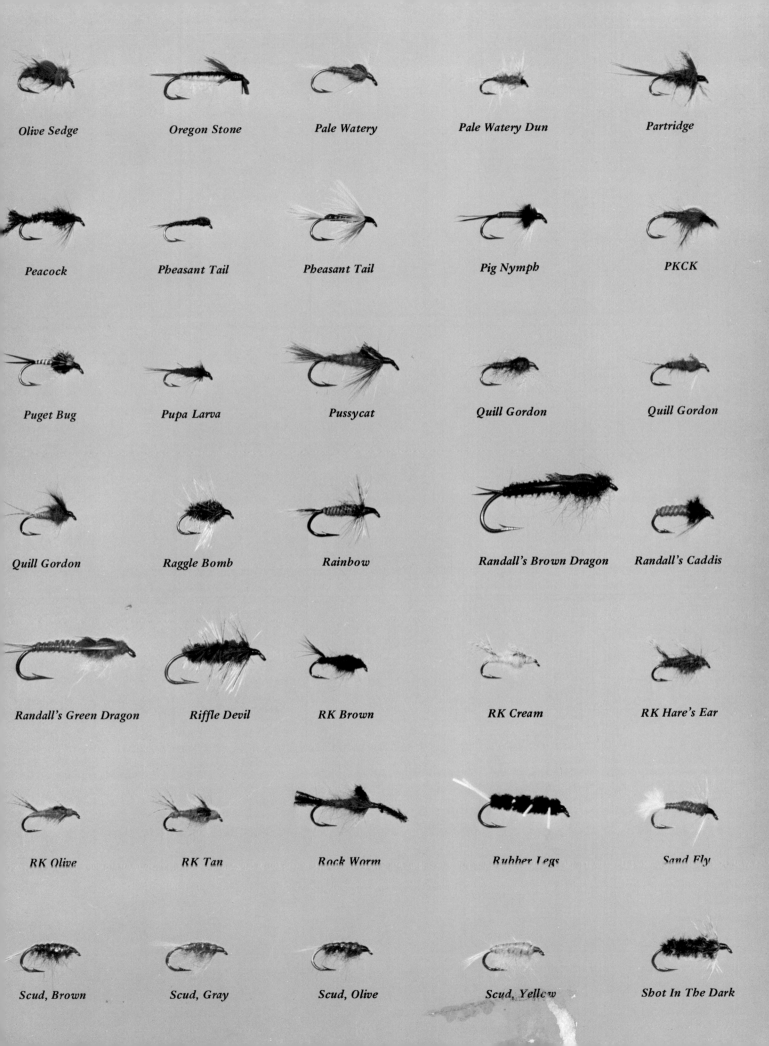

Olive Sedge	Oregon Stone	Pale Watery	Pale Watery Dun	Partridge
Peacock	Pheasant Tail	Pheasant Tail	Pig Nymph	PKCK
Puget Bug	Pupa Larva	Pussycat	Quill Gordon	Quill Gordon
Quill Gordon	Raggle Bomb	Rainbow	Randall's Brown Dragon	Randall's Caddis
Randall's Green Dragon	Riffle Devil	RK Brown	RK Cream	RK Hare's Ear
RK Olive	RK Tan	Rock Worm	Rubber Legs	Sand Fly
Scud, Brown	Scud, Gray	Scud, Olive	Scud, Yellow	Shot In The Dark

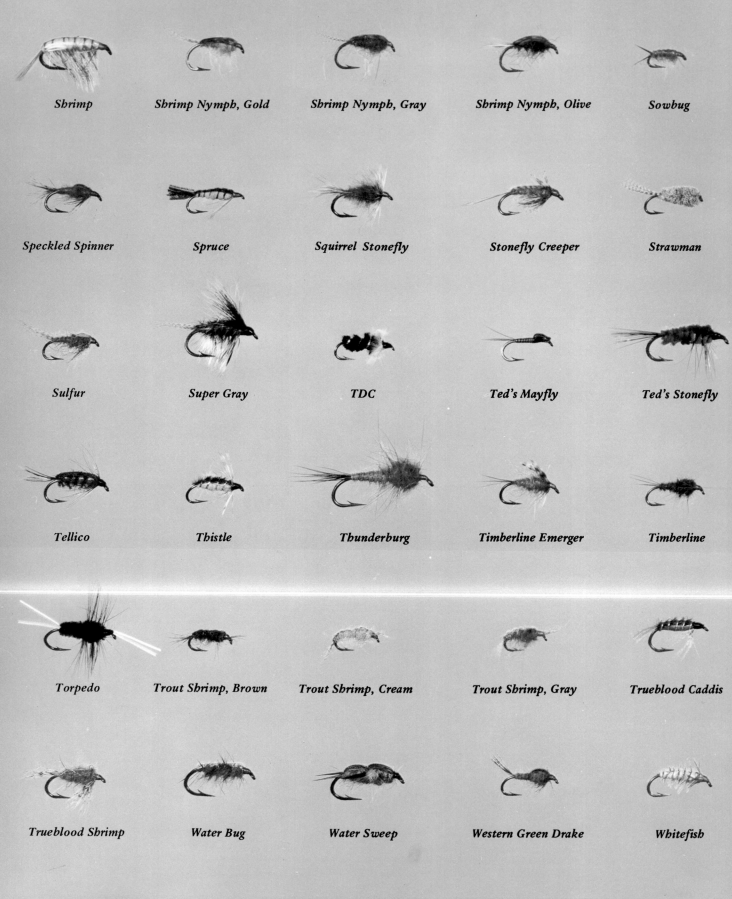

Shrimp Shrimp Nymph, Gold Shrimp Nymph, Gray Shrimp Nymph, Olive Sowbug

Speckled Spinner Spruce Squirrel Stonefly Stonefly Creeper Strawman

Sulfur Super Gray TDC Ted's Mayfly Ted's Stonefly

Tellico Thistle Thunderburg Timberline Emerger Timberline

Torpedo Trout Shrimp, Brown Trout Shrimp, Cream Trout Shrimp, Gray Trueblood Caddis

Trueblood Shrimp Water Bug Water Sweep Western Green Drake Whitefish

Whit Nymph, Black Yellow Midge Pupa Zug Bug

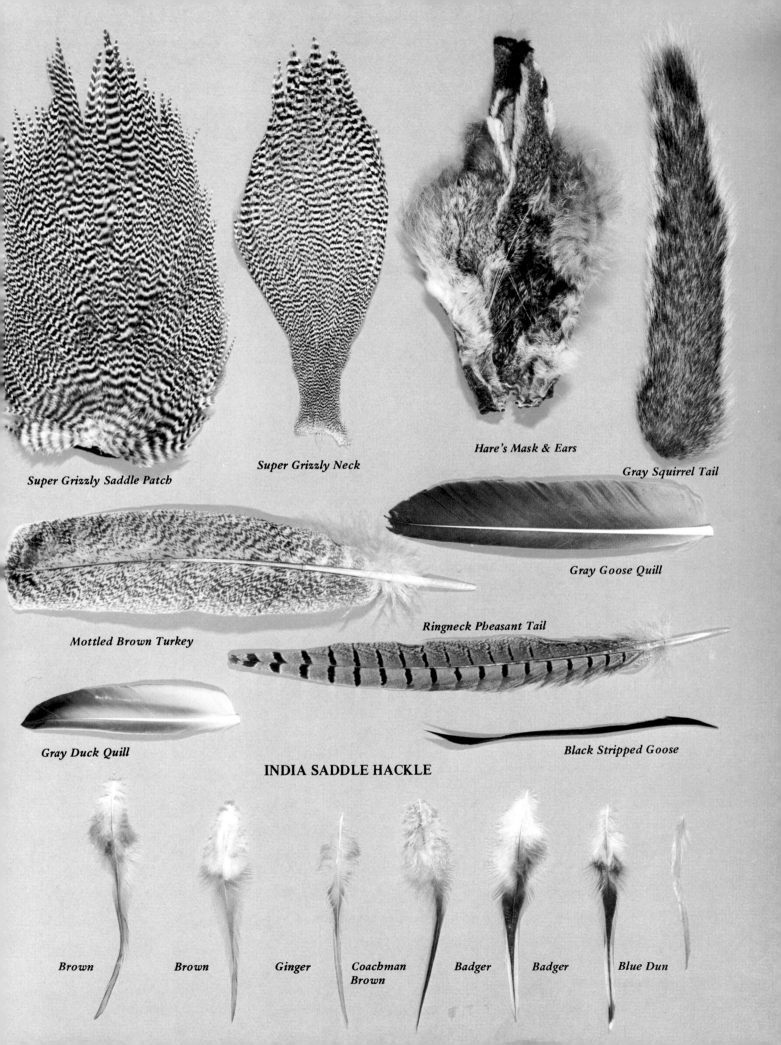

Super Grizzly Saddle Patch

Super Grizzly Neck

Hare's Mask & Ears

Gray Squirrel Tail

Gray Goose Quill

Mottled Brown Turkey

Ringneck Pheasant Tail

Gray Duck Quill

Black Stripped Goose

INDIA SADDLE HACKLE

Brown   Brown   Ginger   Coachman Brown   Badger   Badger   Blue Dun

Bronze Mallard *Natural Mallard* *Mallard Dyed Wood Duck* *Teal* *Dark Partridge* *Light Partridge* *Moose Body Hair*

Otter *Beaver* *Muskrat* *Dyed Rabbit*

Ginger Seal *Yellow Seal* *Green Seal* *Claret Seal* *Cream Seal* *Brown Seal* *Seal and Otter Mix* *Matted Hare's Ear*

Peacock Sword

Peacock Herl

Ostrich

Floss

Moblon

Polly Yarn

Chenille